The Bankruptcy Alternative

The Bankruptcy Alternative

CLOSE YOUR BUSINESS YOUR WAY,

WITHOUT BANKRUPTCY.

SAVE TIME, SAVE MONEY, SAVE YOUR SANITY!

BRUCE BOWLER

Printed in the United States of America.
Cover and interior design: 1106 Design

Publisher: Bowler Enterprises, Inc.
2175 South Jasmine Street, #105
Denver, CO 80222-5700

www.brucebowler.com
info@brucebowler.com

Publisher's Cataloging-in-Publication
(Provided by Quality Books, Inc.)

Bowler, Bruce, author.
The bankruptcy alternative : close your business your way, without bankruptcy : save time, save money, save your sanity! / by Bruce Bowler.

pages cm

LCCN 2017901142

ISBN 978-0-9986328-0-3 (hardcover)
ISBN 978-0-9986328-1-0 (paperback)
ISBN 978-0-9986328-2-7 (ePub)

1. Liquidation—United States—Case studies. 2. Plant shutdowns—United States—Management—Case studies. 3. Business failures—United States—Case studies. 4. Bowler, Bruce. I. Title.

HD2747.B69 2017 658.1'66
QBI17-776

We are all of us not merely liable to fear, we are also prone to be afraid of being afraid, and the conquering of fear produces exhilaration. . . . The contrast between the previous apprehension and the present relief and feeling of security promotes a self-confidence that is the very father and mother of courage.

MALCOLM GLADWELL

DAVID AND GOLIATH

UNDERDOGS, MISFITS, AND THE ART OF BATTLING GIANTS

MEMORANDUM

To: *The Reader*

From: *The Author*

Subject: *Why I wrote* The Bankruptcy Alternative

From time to time as I labored over this work of writing a book on the events surrounding the closure of my business, I wondered, "Why did you undertake the writing of this book?"

I had this strong feeling that I wanted—even needed—to share it with others. As I pondered why, these are the questions that I posed to myself, and my answers:

"Was it to cleanse yourself of bad stuff that might have built up inside of you as you went through the processes of closing the business, selling assets, and paying off debts?"

Maybe, although at times it was very emotionally hard to do—to relive the many experiences and slog through it all again. But, nonetheless, a good cleansing may well have been a nice side benefit.

"Was it to share the most unbelievable story of this epic odyssey with the world?"

Well, absolutely!

"Was it to share the principles I discovered and the tools I used along the way with others, with the intent that it may help them in the event they encountered something similar in their own lives?"

You bet.

"Was it to expose readers to a different side of all those entrepreneurial business books? To give encouragement and hope when things seem most dire? And to tell people that, despite all of our best efforts for our business, sometimes the best option is to shut it down?"

Yes. Yes. And yes.

Okay, then. Let's get after it!

CONTENTS

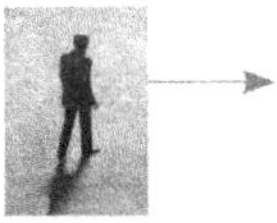

INTRODUCTION

A very long time ago, a young man was put into a leadership role of great visibility, authority, and responsibility. As he was in the midst of struggling with how he was going to be able to handle it all, an older and wiser man who had carried that same position for many years came to him, put his arm around him as they started to take a walk, and said:

"My boy, sometimes you just have to walk into the darkness and pull the light in after you."

What great counsel that turned out to be.

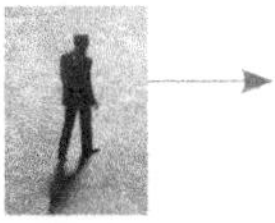

Preface

THE DAY OF DECISION

There is a time to quit.

There. I've written it. Quit.

Are you kidding me!?! Quit?!?

You can't imagine how hard it was to write this word down. All of the multitude of motivational commandments never to give up, to tie a knot in the end of the rope and hang on, and on, and on, make me feel like a traitor to persistence and courage and being an American and all the things that have been driven into me and have become a part of me and who I am and have been for so much of my life.

Yet, when faced with the circumstances I was faced with on September 16, 2009, quitting was really the courageous thing to do. It was the right thing to do. Without question (although certainly not without doubt), it had to be done. That day I clearly remembered the story of walking into the darkness, and as I made the decision to close the company, I felt I stepped off into a black hole in space. I just hoped that I would be able to pull the light in after me.

Now for the story.

Chapter 1

THE BEGINNING

In January of 2000, I made the decision to start a new business. In spite of the things that would have said "Don't do this" (like the gem of wisdom from the great book *The Richest Man in Babylon* that so wisely counsels one not to get into a business that you know nothing about), I rose to the challenge presented to me by a dear friend of so many years and bought the leftover pieces of a custom-apparel manufacturing business and started our new business known as Phoenix Custom Apparel.

And, over nine and a half years, it never made a profit. Until the year I closed it down. And, that was only because we closed it down before year's end.

There really was some thought and reasoning put behind the decision to open up a new business that I had absolutely no knowledge about. Matter of fact, I had a fair amount of experience doing just that sort of thing.

In 1955, drag racing got into my bloodstream. I had started racing while in high school, and built and raced cars at the drag strip. It changed my life drastically.

In 1958, while still in high school, I also began a lengthy career in the mortgage-banking industry, working for my dad at his mortgage company. I stayed with Dad for some ten years, during which time I got married, started a family, graduated from high school and college, and really established a solid foundation in my chosen profession of being a mortgage banker.

But, in my personal time, I continued with my passion for drag racing; I even started up an advertising and race-car booking agency with a friend of mine, which we conducted in the evenings and weekends.

One day Dad called me into his office and pointed out that "my portion" of the company phone bill (which I reimbursed him for) was larger than the company portion. He suggested that I needed to decide what I was going to do with my life. I agreed with him, and sent off a resume to the National Hot Rod Association.

I thought I'd see if there might be a place for me with the sport's premier sanctioning body that fathered the sport of drag racing. I had been part of the Certification Team of the West Central Division of NHRA and had done quite a lot of announcing at events all over our Division, so I was no novice to drag racing and the NHRA.

Shortly thereafter, in the fall of 1968, I was offered and quickly accepted the position of Northwest Division Director of the National Hot Rod Association. A Valvoline contact told me how great Vancouver, Washington, was, so I flew up to Portland, rented a car, drove around Vancouver, found a beautiful home in a wooded development, signed a contract to purchase the home, and flew back to Denver.

I put our home in Denver on the market, then uprooted my wife and three small children, and we took off for the Pacific Northwest. As soon as we got a motel room, I took my wife and children to see what our new home looked like. Fortunately, they all loved it, so we closed on the purchase and moved into our new home in Vancouver.

There we were. In a brand-new part of the country we had never been in before, in a home my wife had never seen until we were up there, and in a brand-new industry. I was now responsible for drag racing, NHRA style, for the four-corner states of Washington, Oregon, Idaho, and Montana; the three Canadian Provinces of Saskatchewan, Alberta, and British Columbia; and Alaska, with the task of bringing back the lost prominence of the NHRA with the track operators and the racers.

Thus, from the very structured environment of mortgage banking, I jumped into the emerging world of drag racing. I became one of seven men who grew and officiated over this new, exciting sport. Wow! Can you imagine taking this leap of faith and getting a job in the sport that was your passion? Adrenaline was racing through me faster than nitro-methane through a top-fuel dragster.

However, I quickly learned that this new life and position was not easy. A story will clarify this statement.

It was the spring of 1969 and my first Division Event as the newly presiding Division Director. We were holding this event at a relatively new race track just outside of Boise, Idaho, by the name of Firebird Raceway, with new ownership and crew. Sound like a recipe for trouble?

My wife (who ran the Timing Tower crew) and I got there on a Wednesday to get things set up and to go around to the media to do marketing for the event, etc. The time trials began early Saturday morning, to qualify the cars entered for the limited car fields that would compete in the final eliminations on Sunday afternoon. What I was soon to learn was that shutting off time trials to get ready to assemble the final fields was going to be one of the most difficult activities of my division director life.

All throughout Saturday's time trials, I kept looking for the Northwest's biggest name in drag racing, Jerry "The King" Ruth, who campaigned his nationally renowned Top Fuel Dragster from his stable in Seattle. He was a pretty spunky guy—as a driver of a car capable of going faster than 250 miles per hour in a quarter mile should be—and had no difficulty thinking highly of himself. This was the first Division Event of the year, and one that would be important to a Divisional and National Champion like The King.

Well, finally JR showed up at about eleven o'clock on Sunday morning. He took his time unloading the car from his trailer, and getting it all ready for a run. Then he nonchalantly pulled it into the staging lanes, just in time to be able to make one qualifying pass. After all, he was The King, and one pass would certainly be all he would need to qualify for the quickest eight qualifiers in his class.

Everything was going fine. He got up to the line just as we were coming up to the cutoff time. His crew fired up the car. Everything was shipshape. He did his burnout. Looked great.

He backed up the car with hand signals from his crew so he would stay in his tracks, stopped his car behind the starting line as he should, put it in his one forward gear, and began to pull up to the starting line to make his one qualifying pass.

Perfect.

Oh, no! As the car was moving into the staging beams, one of the members of his crew who was behind the race car, accidentally snagged the release wire hooked to the container the parachute was packed carefully into, and the parachute popped out of the container and fell onto the ground!!!

Oh, crap.

Everyone was stunned. The crew frantically started stuffing that parachute into the driver's seat, right behind where JR was strapped in.

What?!? Somehow, JR is going to blast full tilt down that dragstrip and, at the finish line, going 250-plus miles per hour, reach behind him and throw the parachute out of the seat and get that car stopped?!?

Not on my watch.

I was up in the Timing Tower and reached over to the "kill switch" on the Timing Tree activator, and hit the switch. Immediately the red lights began flashing on the Timing Tree on the starting line, and JR knew that this run was over.

He killed the engine, unbuckled the safety harnesses, and stood up in the car. Then he took off his helmet and looked up at the Timing Tower. And I looked down at him standing in his car.

He got out and headed my way. I left the Tower and headed his way. It was the perfect reenactment of the Gunfight at the OK Corral. I was sick to my stomach.

When we were face to face, JR said, "You're going to let me make another qualifying pass—right?"

I responded, "You know, JR, everyone has been here for almost two days doing qualifying runs to get into the field. The time for qualifying has run out. There's no way I can let you make another pass."

I'll hand it to JR. He turned around, took his car and crew back into the pits, loaded up, and left the track before our first round of eliminations started.

That did not feel good. But it had to be done.

However, I can tell you that, at our next Division Event in Bremerton, Washington, The King was first in line at the entrance gate when Julie and I pulled up to open up the track on Saturday morning. And he qualified Number One at that event—and set a new national record for Top Fuel Dragster.

I experienced great personal growth that can only come from being responsible for making decisions that are tough ones. Not long after having my first couple of Division Events under my belt, I remember lying in bed one night with tears in my eyes, after having had to make and stand behind the many difficult decisions that I found came with the job, wondering why in the world I had left the comfortable life we'd had back in Denver, working for my dad and pretty well embedded into my chosen profession— which I was pretty good at.

So, naturally, the thought that came to my mind was just to quit and go back to Denver. Be comfortable again. This new career was just too hard.

But, that quiet voice came to me in that moment and, as clearly as someone speaking to me from across the kitchen table, said: "If you quit this job now and go back home to your dad, you will never amount to a hill of beans. But, if you will suck it up and see this through, once you get to the point where you think you have successfully done what you need to do, then you can resign and go on to whatever you want."

I made a covenant with myself in that moment: *I would not quit until I had won.* It took almost three years to get to the point where I felt I had done what I was hired to do, that I had accomplished what the Division needed to have done, and that I could leave with my head held high. And when I got to that point, I resigned and took my family back home. My tour of duty was done.

It made me my own man and changed my life completely.

As a follow-up to my relationship with Jerry Ruth, when I had announced I was leaving my position and the Northwest, I went to see JR at his home, where he kept his race car. We had developed a pretty good relationship since that rough start, and I wanted to tell him goodbye.

JR told me that, while he did not agree with all of my decisions, he did respect me for not backing down once I had made one. "In fact," he said, "you may not know it, but you have a nickname in the Division."

"Really," I said. "I've never had a nickname before. What is it?"

"Little Caesar."

We both laughed, my chest a little more expanded. Thank you, JR.

We moved back to Denver, and I spent the next twenty-seven years in various aspects of the mortgage-banking industry. Within that time, I rose to the position of Senior Vice President of the Mortgage Banking Division of Van Schaack & Company, the largest real estate sales / development / mortgage-banking firm in Colorado. Following a brief stint in the home-building industry, my wife and I took out a second mortgage on our home and purchased half interest in Universal Lending Corporation, one of the locally owned-and-operated mortgage companies in town. During that fourteen-year partnership with Pete Lansing, we grew the business from its loan volume of $32 million in 1984 to a volume approaching $1 billion a year, and we had become a real player in the Denver market.

And, after nearly forty years in the mortgage-banking business, I decided I needed a change. I felt I had had a successful career, but, honestly, I was bored, and tired of the business.

So, in the summer of 1998, I sold my half of the business back to my business partner for a tidy sum and did what anyone with my background would have done. I did a burnout and went back to drag racing—as a driver.

I went back full-time, as a semi-professional with three sons and a daughter as the bulk of my crew, driving a top-alcohol dragster that went from 0 to 271 miles per hour in a quarter mile. Naturally, I had chosen the race car that was deemed to be the most difficult combination of a normally aspirated, nitro-methane-fuel-powered motor, but it was an awesome machine and could cover the 1,320 feet in 5.3 seconds from the starting line to the finish line.

Sure, it took us two years of experimentation and blowing up motors just to get the car to go from the starting line to the finish line under power. Sure, it was the side of drag racing that I knew about only from amateur-level tinkering in high school. And, there I go again: getting into something that I didn't know much about, but stepping up to the challenge of accomplishing something for myself and my team through the blood, sweat, and tears of continuing to turn over every rock until you find the solution.

You'd think I'd have learned. Oh, did I tell you? Walt Disney is probably my biggest hero, and one of my all-time favorite books is *Running From Safety* by Richard Bach.

A dear friend of mine told me one time: "Good judgment comes from experience; experience comes from bad judgment."

How accurate is that statement?!

Well, over time, we came from being nobody on the track to being fairly well-known and recognized as a tough competitor. In 2000, we were ranked # 8 in the nation in our category. We won a fiercely fought battle to take the title of Division 5 Champion in the Federal Mogul Dragster category and, in August of 2001, we won our first and only National Event title in Brainerd, Minnesota. We were now Champions, and were finally able to have the coveted NHRA Champions Jackets made by our company, for our own team members. Sweet.

During our campaign as professional racers, seeing all the money I was pouring in to the operation to keep us on the track, I said to my son Scott, who was my crew chief and worked full-time doing that, "We need to have some kind of business to generate some income."

And, like so many things in life, when you put it out into the universe, the universe responds. Not two days after making that statement, in through the front door of our leased racing facility came my old and long-time friend, who had really ushered me into the business side of the sport of drag racing, Jim Tibbitts.

Jim ran, owned, and operated various businesses associated with automobile racing in all its venues, and he was ready to get out of his custom-apparel-manufacturing business.

Jim had a contract with the National Hot Rod Association to manufacture all of their Winner's Jackets, which NHRA gave to every winning driver of every National Event. And, with the number of national events and the number of racing categories they ran at each event, that came to a delivery of some 200 jackets a year. Not enough to start—or continue—a business, but when you build in the opportunity for the winning drivers to order additional Champion Jackets for members of their crew or family, etc., all of a sudden, that potential goes up to maybe 1,400 jackets per year.

Then add to that the sale and manufacturing of heavily decorated, embroidered team uniforms, etc., and now you have just come up with an exciting and supportable reason for the creation of this new business, buying the materials and equipment of the existing business, and taking on the existing clients, including the NHRA. After all, from my time as a Division Director and now as a full-time, semi-professional NHRA drag racer, I knew the market and the players very well.

How insatiable—this challenge of picking up the pieces to build something new, committing money, and time, and dedication to it. Just think of what can be created here. As you can see, one could make some pretty strong arguments that it really made some sense to do this, and the ingredients also made it pretty irresistible.

So, I drove down to El Paso, Texas, with Jim. We toured his operation and saw he had his people, materials, and sewing machines in an old industrial building with dirt floors. We went to lunch, and I said to Jim, "You can't really manufacture apparel with dirt floors, can you?" He replied, "Of course not. We'll need new space." And, after a moment, I said, "Well, let's go look for some." And with that statement, the decision was made to purchase Jim's company.

In February of 2000, that fiery mythological bird rose from the ashes. Phoenix Custom Apparel was born.

Chapter 2

THE "S" CURVE OF BUSINESS

Before I go on, let me share an important piece of information regarding the reasoning behind anyone going into business for themselves and what he or she is likely to experience after having made the decision to start it up.

It's called The "S" Curve of business.

The "S" Curve of Business

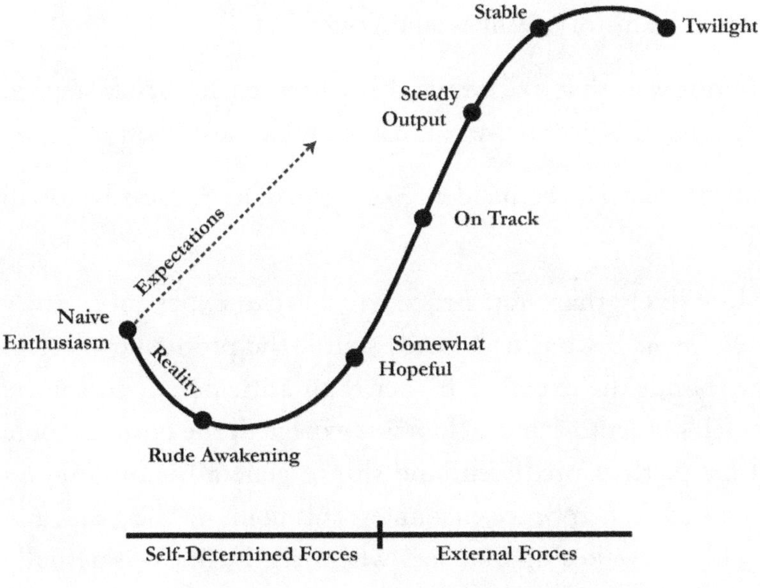

As a first prerequisite, the would-be entrepreneur (let's call this one "Bruce") must have some reason in his or her mind that this business endeavor is the greatest thing since sliced bread, and that he is going to do very well at whatever that business is all about. Otherwise, why would Bruce start this business?!

In the "S" Curve, we call that beginning point in the graph "Naive Enthusiasm." Anyone who has started up a business—or any venture for that matter, be it a marriage, buying a home, going out west, pretty much any kind of new thing—has experienced this euphoric feeling that gives them not only the incentive but also the courage to take such a step. Optimism and adrenaline kick in, and everything is possible.

And, naturally, once Bruce opened the door to his newly founded business, his expectations were that the business would just take off like a rocket ship to the moon and that the rest would be history. Why wouldn't it?

Thus it was, that like every other entrepreneur, Bruce stepped right into his own naive enthusiasm with the highest of hopes.

Unfortunately, the incidence of immediate success is not all that high.

More likely than not, Bruce will start to experience reality therapy as his business heads south, the profits nowhere to be found, the expenses higher than anticipated, customers much harder to acquire than was expected, the business more difficult than predicted, and things generally not going as planned. When Bruce encounters this point on the graph and suddenly wakes up and sees where the business is actually headed, Bruce has found himself in the realm known as the "Rude Awakening."

Once aware of his predicament, Bruce now has a decision to make: "Do I jump off this sinking ship, or do I step up to the plate and work harder, invest more, change some things, etc., and hope like crazy that it works and that this business comes around?"

Many bail out at this point. Some don't. Bruce didn't.

Issues were analyzed, changes made, and efforts to save the business were increased. *After all, let's give this business a real chance to make it.*

So Bruce does these things and more, and what happens many times with businesses happened to Bruce, and things start coming around and actually head in the direction Bruce was hoping to see all along. With that uptick in results, Bruce has just found himself in the position of now being "Somewhat Hopeful," as the curve on the graph is finally heading in the right direction.

If Bruce continues to make good decisions and the planets start to come into alignment, Bruce could well find himself "On Track" and at the helm of a business that is actually starting to make it and become what Bruce had dreamed of. From there, if all goes well, the business climbs into the "Steady Output" stage and beyond. You can see where the graph goes from there. We won't cover the top part of the graph, as it could be the substance of a whole other book.

Basically, there's the graph in all its simplicity. However, nothing operates in its own vacuum, including the creation and growth of a business. So, let's add just two more of the many factors that will interact with this "S" Curve model and impact Bruce's business path.

The first of these factors is called "Self-Determined Forces." These are the things that Bruce can do, is willing to do, has influence over, and needs to be involved in, all of which will have a lot to do with how this company performs and where it will go. We can't assume Bruce will be proficient in this arena, but let's hope that he is or that, with enough time, effort, and money, he can become proficient to help this business be a success.

The second of these factors is called "External Forces." These are the factors outside of the business and the business entrepreneur that Bruce has no control over. Maybe the industry Bruce has picked goes through a major shift, or new regulations create havoc, the prices of his materials triple, some new product comes into the market that makes his obsolete, etc. On the other hand, perhaps it's more than just a microcosm occurrence within his industry. Maybe it's a national economic situation that has just knocked everyone for a loop—or maybe even a global issue that has raised up its ugly head. These forces are limitless, and any or all of them can have a huge impact on how that business does.

With all that being set forth, realize that Bruce felt he had assembled enough evidence to convince himself that the creation of his new business was not only justified but that it would be all he envisioned to be a successful and profitable investment on its own, and further, to be able to provide enough bottom-line income to support Bruce's other activities.

Thus, it was, that like every other entrepreneur, Bruce stepped right into his own naive enthusiasm when he told Jimmy: "Well, let's go look for some space to rent."

On January 27, 2000, we filed our Articles of Incorporation for Phoenix Motorsports Apparel Corporation with the Colorado Secretary of State, and were officially in business as a Colorado corporation. We later filed our "doing business as" name, and became known as Phoenix Custom Apparel.

Chapter 3

THE MIDDLE

I was now a manufacturer of custom-designed and domestically produced apparel.

We rented space in the heart of El Paso, setting up a full cut-and-sew operation there. With the production staff in El Paso and the owners and upper management located in Denver, we began manufacturing product for our existing customers.

It didn't take long, nor did you need to be a genius, to figure out that this arrangement was not going to work out well. So, after consulting with my wife, we began looking for a production facility in Denver. We ended up purchasing a twenty-thousand-square-foot office warehouse building on 40th Avenue just west of Colorado Boulevard, and we moved all of our equipment and inventory into our new facility.

None of our employees in El Paso wanted to move to Denver, so we took on an experienced production staff of people who had just been let go from another racing apparel company that had been closed, and we didn't miss a beat.

It was an exciting experience, to say the least. But the rude awakening was brutal. Reality therapy showed up quickly as we incurred a loss in the mid-six figures in that first year of operation in the Denver facility. We had too much space and too many employees for the amount of business we were generating, and, from that moment on, it was the constant battle of studying, worrying, making decisions on what changes to implement, etc., all with the unyielding conviction that there was a way to make this company profitable.

Over the years, we added on to our company structure to the point that we had full capabilities to produce embroidered products; the emerging sublimated apparel; create our own patterns; manufacture shirts, pants, and jackets; and manufacture SFI-rated firesuits for race car drivers. Fittingly, I was the test pilot for team uniforms and drivers' firesuits, trying out new fabrics and design features out on the race track as we continued to campaign the dragster under the Phoenix Custom Apparel banner.

We became the Official Uniform of the National Hot Rod Association and of many other sanctioning bodies for racing of all venues. We were very visible, and business grew accordingly, to the point where we experienced difficulties keeping up with demand. We had garnered high-profile customers like Michael Andretti and his five Indy 500 teams, and drag-racing team greats like Joe Amato, Kenny Bernstein, Forest Lucas, and many others for whom we were manufacturing striking, sublimated crew shirts and other products. One time, all of the crew uniform shirts worn by racing team members and racetrack officials who were on the Starting Line of the Mile High Nationals had been manufactured by our company. Our quality was top notch, our delivery was on time, and we were well respected.

We had a production team that was outstanding, with a family atmosphere. We had state-of-the-art, computerized patternmaking equipment; with computerized digital graphics capability for all of our graphic artists; embroidery and sublimation capabilities; in-house Lean Manufacturing training for personnel; a High-Impact Language Training program designed by a former professor of the University of Denver to teach English to those who needed help, that was taught by members of our own executive committee; and a spirit of helping one another in every aspect of business and personal life.

However, even though we experienced a huge increase in worker productivity, producing much more business with a lot less employees, the margins were always thin. And even though we finally were able to make monthly profits from time to time, huge seasonal drops in orders during the summer and fall, when racing teams already had purchased their team apparel for the year, consistently denied us a profit at the end of a year. It was nowhere to be found.

I felt that we had done everything we could to enhance our "Self-Determined Forces."

To say it was discouraging would be a huge understatement. My wife and I were totally committed to making the company work, even to the demise of all of our resources that had come from a lifetime of work, but the future did not look good in 2009.

Chapter 4

THE U.S. ECONOMY TANKS

When I was half-owner of Universal Lending Corporation from 1984 through the summer of 1998, my partner Pete Lansing and I learned some great lessons as our business went through the huge cyclical movements in our volume of mortgage business. One of the great ones was that we really weren't as smart and as invincible as we thought we were. Many a monthly loss took away some awesome profits as we fought through internal and external stumbling blocks, not the least of which was the horrendous business cycles caused by movements in interest rates.

The other great lesson we learned with those business cycles is that, while a business owner can wish all he or she wants for future business volume and can easily make estimates of future business and justify acting accordingly, the one glaring fact that ultimately comes and smacks you in the face is this: "The Market Is the Market!"

"The Market Is the Market" means that you MUST lift up your head and take a look at the business environment that you and the nation are currently in and come to grips with the reality that what you are experiencing is just what it is. Any forecasting you are going to do in making your business decisions absolutely must take into account what is currently taking place; then you must realistically make a determination of what will be the most likely business scenario resulting from that business environment and make necessary adjustments to your company.

Period.

When we ignored this business principle, we got hammered. When we used it wisely, we did well.

When I saw the terrible, worldwide financial crisis that came from the mortgage meltdown and its impact on housing prices and how that was snowballing through the entire national and global economy, my biggest recollection was how grateful I was that I was no longer in the mortgage business and had gone into another industry.

After all, I was in a totally different industry now, and either subconsciously or, perhaps more accurately, ignorantly, I did not think that the racing industry that our apparel business was so connected to, was subject to the same ups and downs of the nation's economy that were having such a devastating effect on the mortgage industry.

I could not have been more wrong.

It wasn't until the summer of 2009 when I attended a special NHRA Major Sponsor Meeting in Sonoma, California, for all the sponsor companies that I realized my mistake. In addition to Phoenix Custom Apparel being there as the Official Uniform of NHRA, companies like POWERADE/Coca Cola, Fram, AAA, Goodyear, Valvoline, and ESPN were participants. It was a very high-powered group of companies and representatives in attendance, all gathered to not only hear from the NHRA on what their future plans were, but also, even more importantly, to give the participating sponsors the ability to share with each other what was going on with them, and have close interaction on what the future looked like, and how to address the then-current drop in business that everyone was experiencing.

ESPN made a wonderfully insightful presentation on what had been happening with their business and shared an insight they came up with through their research of "What happened?"

They, too, had experienced a significant drop in business. Their representative told us that, in trying to figure out why, they had gone over all the economic events through the past number of years, trying to see if there was some incident that they could point to that was the moment that the economy turned totally to crap and the freefall began.

From their analysis, he told us that they felt they could clearly state that the one event that was the dead giveaway that we were all in big trouble occurred on September 15, 2008.

That was the day Lehman Brothers filed for bankruptcy.

The federal government had made the decision that they were not going to try to keep that financial-services institution afloat, and the largest bankruptcy filing in U.S. history hit the streets.

And when I listened to what ESPN shared, I realized that it was not just Phoenix Custom Apparel that had seen a significant downturn in business, but everyone. Everywhere. In a real way, that made me feel better, relieved that I hadn't done something wrong but that we were all feeling the downturn because of the external forces we found ourselves in.

However, now comes the rub.

I had not paid attention to it. I did not look up and study the nation's business activity. And I failed to understand that this economic disaster was already having a huge impact on the auto-racing industry.

Chapter 5

THE BAD FEELING

I sensed the end may be nearing, with my trip to the 2009 NHRA Winternationals in Pomona, California, in early February. This was the first major drag-racing event of the year for the industry. It was the event where everyone always showed up in their shiny, new team uniforms, with their shiny, new cars, and everything was presented in the best possible light for the beginning of the new racing season. It was where optimism, enthusiasm, excitement, and expectation levels were at their highest.

It rained.

Incessantly.

And, walking through the pit area, looking at the decimated ranks of the racing community, and feeling the depression of the participants, it was more than gloomy.

Standing near the Nitro Mall Tent, in the rain, in two inches of water, talking to a long-time associate of mine about how his sales of racing equipment/supplies was going, it got much worse. He told me how so many teams had gone from multiple racecar teams in their operation down to one, or maybe two, and what that meant in terms of his sales of items like cylinder sleeves and head gaskets, etc. He told me that most teams still had lots of that stuff available from when they started cutting back on the number of cars they were putting on the track, as sponsors began going away. All of what I saw and heard confirmed everything I was feeling.

I could sense that black hole, cold and suffocating, inching ever closer to me. I was sick to my stomach at that event, and, on my way home, I sent out an urgent message to my top leaders at Phoenix Custom Apparel to meet me the next day.

Don't quit.

When we met, we talked about how slim orders were going, what I experienced at the Winternationals, and, most importantly, what we were going to do to try to reverse our sales and get some activity generated. Because things were so tight with the racing teams, some of our customers were jumping ship and going to other suppliers for as little as $8 per shirt less. And that was happening with core customers, the ones that had been with us for a long time, the ones that we had bent over backwards for to take care of when they got themselves in a jam and needed superlative service to pull them out of it. We were also seeing teams switching to product manufactured overseas, which cut their prices by way more than $8 per shirt. Add to that, the orders we were receiving were smaller, because the teams had less crew members than prior years.

Don't quit.

In spite of everything, we circled the wagons and put together an overall, comprehensive plan of action regarding every single facet of our business, including securing short-term financing to bring it around. And every step was complete with a deadline for showing improvement. We were making a stand, pooling every resource in the fight to stay afloat.

Don't quit.

Our first-quarter sales proved just how bad it was. This was the critical sales period of the year, as it set the tone for the rest of the busy season, which encompassed the first six months of each year, after which sales dropped like a rock. It wasn't pretty. Volume had dropped by 50 percent from the previous year's First Quarter Sales. Bummer.

Don't quit.

And, fortunately, things did improve. We put together our short-term financing but didn't have to use more than about 30 percent of it to keep us afloat; some great orders that came in during the second quarter really carried us well. I used some of those funds to pay off the short-term debt, and then, breathing easier with that obligation gone, I continued to look at approaching sales during our "down time" and what that would mean to the future of our company.

But, honestly, what did the future really look like?

Perhaps there should be another place somewhere in that "S" Curve entitled "Unrealistic Optimism." This is where things are not going as planned; losses continue despite hard work and planning. But the entrepreneur still hangs on to the thought that it couldn't possibly be that maybe this business is just not going to work. This also ties back into not paying attention to or dealing with that principle spoken of earlier that says, "The Market Is the Market."

When this happens, we can see how easy it is for the business owner to get into a death spiral. The owner hears that whisper that says: "If I can just keep this going for another three months, I can find a new customer who will turn this puppy around …"; or, "If we can just make it through December and get into our busy season again …."

Time after time, we ignore, or fail to admit, that the business is simply not going to make it. "Reality therapy" is about to take place.

That's exactly what happened to me. There were a lot of forces that kept me in that death spiral. I really felt if I kept searching and trying, I could figure out how to fix it and make this business profitable. I really felt that there was a pony in there somewhere. Look at all the wonderful employees who were depending upon the company for their livelihood and the relationships that had been built around what we did. Look at the great product we produced, the awesome customers we had, and all the affiliations we had put together with sanctioning bodies all over the country. How can this not work? Plus, we were out there campaigning a dragster with Phoenix Custom Apparel all over the truck and trailer and body of the race car. How can we let all this fail?

So, I continued to risk the family resources that we had built over forty years of blood, sweat, and tears. I had sold my interest in Universal Lending and had millions in the bank. Literally. But it didn't take long for that to start eroding. The money was disappearing faster and faster until I got a handle on the business and made the changes we made. But, that wasn't enough, so when our accountant made us aware of an income tax "fund" that had been created by what we paid the IRS when we sold our interest in the mortgage company, we tapped into that tax fund, and it was very helpful in keeping things afloat. Then came tapping into our retirement funds. Then tapping into the cash value of life-insurance policies. We were running out of sources of funds, and so it happened that, to meet payroll, I found myself cashing in the gold coins that I had accumulated, capped off by selling the gold Rolex watch that was acquired back in my mortgage-banking days.

We were out of money. The resources the company had left were very, very limited.

At least no one could say we didn't give it our all. We absolutely did.

Chapter 6

THRESHOLDS AND WINDOWS

In life, we are presented a series of thresholds and windows.

Thresholds are when you stand there in front of an opportunity and make a decision to cross over or not cross over the threshold that is in front of you. It may mean getting a new job, or getting married, or driving a race car, starting a new business, etc. And, you either decide to step over that threshold into what is awaiting you when you make that step, or you don't, and you continue with things the way they are. Looking back with the wisdom and benefit of hindsight, sometimes stepping over that threshold is the right thing to do.

Sometimes it's not.

Whether you step over that threshold that is in front of you or not is not the issue here. The issue is that you *will* be presented with thresholds, and decisions *will* have to be made.

Don't fool yourself: Not making a decision is a decision.

Windows are a whole other phenomenon, and they are varied in their characteristics. With our racing operation, we constantly were challenged to have the tune-up close enough to perfection to put our performance "in the window"—that always-sought-after-but-difficult-to-find window. To give you an example, our racing team knew we were NOT in the window when we would make huge, drastic changes in the car's tune-up, but the car performed at exactly the same miserable performance it did the run before, with no improvement or detriment in the outcome.

On the other hand, we knew with certainty we were in the window when the slightest change in any of the multitude of tune-up components would produce a measurable and noticeable change in the performance outcome of the run. And understand, by "slightest," I mean as little as changing the weight on the clutch fingers by the weight of six one-dollar bills.

That's a *performance* window.

There's also an *opportunity* window.

That window is that time period or moment when you can take action on something. It may be that you are searching to buy just the right home, and you see it, and in that moment, it's available. When that window opens up, you'd best be prepared to take action, or you may well miss that window, and the opportunity will slip away. Hesitate too long on buying that special home, and someone else will put it under contract—and it's gone.

Having been blessed throughout my many years with lots of thresholds and lots of windows, I was able to clearly recognize that on the fifteenth of September, 2009, there was a very distinct window that was open. I also recognized that the length of time that window was going to be open was very brief.

Here's what the window was:

I determined that if I closed Phoenix Custom Apparel down *right now*, I would have sufficient funds left to complete all the orders that we had in the system, pay for all the materials that we had purchased, and pay all the salaries and other compensation that was going to be payable to the employees. I also felt that there would very possibly be enough company assets that could be liquidated with sufficient equity to be able to pay off all the company debts.

I also believed that if I did *not* close the company down, right now, and take the actions to clean it all out and begin the liquidation process, that I would be digging myself into a deeper hole to the extent that I would absolutely *not* be able to pay everyone their due, unless our business picked up significantly and enable the company to go forward with some good, strong net profit.

So, the first step was recognizing that there was a window of opportunity in front of us, that it wasn't very wide, and would not be open long.

The next step, then, was to determine if there was anything on the horizon that I or my executives could see that would give us an indication that the business climate was going to get better than what we had experienced so far in 2009. Was it reasonable to expect that our own volume of business was going to pick up, that we could charge more money for our product to increase our profit margin, or to expect anything else that would enhance the outlook for the future?

In various discussions I had with my wife, my executives, our board members (which included the company accountant and the company attorney), plus my own crystal-ball analysis, I found there was very little hope that the business climate was going to improve; as a matter of fact, it really appeared that, if anything, it would get worse. Therefore, to hang on and rely on *hope* and/or *luck* to keep the business afloat would be a serious mistake. And, I had learned over time that, if you have to rely on luck to survive, you are already toast!

With my own analysis completed, and the window open for that brief moment, I came to the realization that closing down the company was not only a very real possibility, but, for the first time, I came to the conclusion that we *absolutely* had to close the business and take advantage of the opportunity this open window was offering us.

I felt that it was time to cross this threshold, step into the darkness, and see if I could pull the light in after me.

Chapter 7

THE END

There is a Time to Pull the Plug

With the realization in my own mind that to close the company down was most likely the right thing to do, I called a meeting for the following day with my trusted Executive Team, which was comprised of my son Matt Bowler, who served as our VP of Art & Design, and my daughter Mary Tennien, who served as our VP of Production. The intent of that meeting was to share with them everything I had studied and all information I had gathered, and then jointly come to a final conclusion on what we should do.

We held that meeting on September 16, and, after due discussion and analysis, without hesitation, we made the unanimous decision to pull the plug on Phoenix Custom Apparel.

We just crossed the threshold and stepped out into the black hole in space.

I want to say here, what a high regard I have for the courage of my Executive Team. By making the decision to close the company, Matt and Mary literally put themselves out of a job.

Matt had just gotten married the month before, and Mary was pregnant. But we were all in harmony that it was the right thing to do, and now that the decision had been made, it was just a matter of figuring out how to do it.

Chapter 8

THE COMPANY CLOSURE STORYBOARD

We immediately began the process of creating the "Closing the Company Down" Storyboard. Yes, *Storyboard*: the process created and used by Walt Disney to produce animated cartoons and movies from the idea concepts to the actual, finished products. That powerful tool had morphed into the creation of a process that was turned into perhaps one of the greatest business tools, providing a way of taking an idea and identifying all the steps necessary to bring that idea to fruition. I have used it constantly since learning it some thirty years ago. Through the storyboarding process, we outlined the closing processes and actions to be taken to accomplish the task. Again, there was no hesitation by my team in storyboarding this action, and, in short order, we had the entire wall in our Conference Room covered with all the "Headers" and their "Subbers" that would soon result in the systematic and successful closure of Phoenix Custom Apparel.

On the next page are photos showing the visual of the Storyboard.

The main topic of the Storyboard was "Closing Down the Company." As we all knew what it was all about, we didn't

PCA CLOSURE STORYBOARD RE-CREATED FROM THE ORIGINAL STORYBOARD CARDS.

Left Side

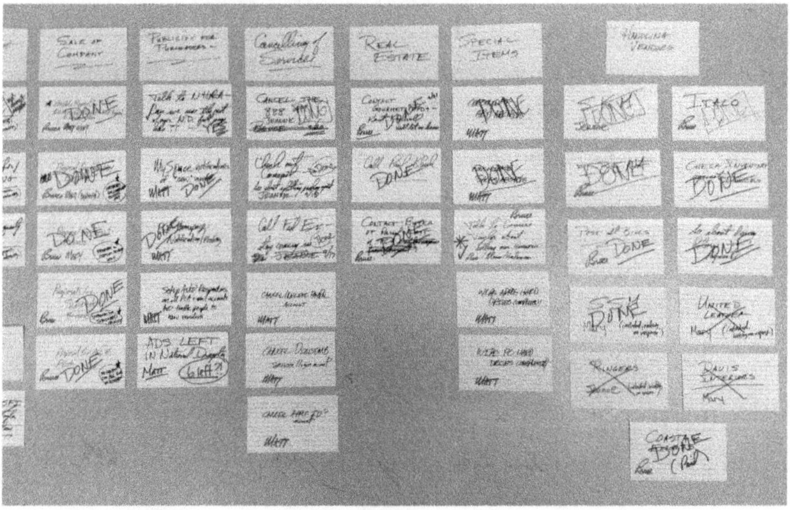

Right Side

go through the formalities of putting the Main Topic up on the wall.

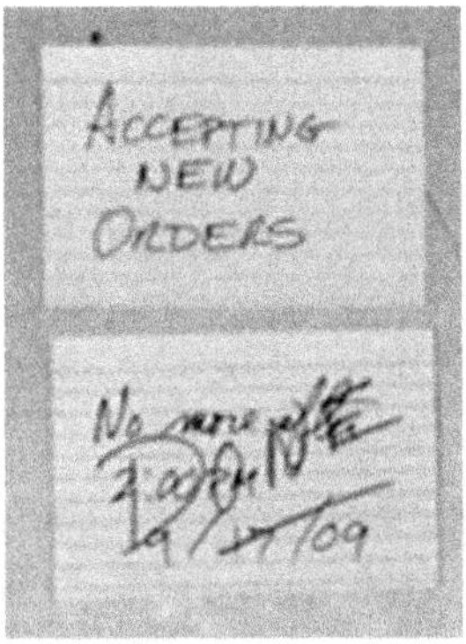

← **Header**

← **Subber**

Enlargement

Each HEADER was to identify each major task that had to be addressed in closing down the company. Each SUBBER was to identify an action item to be performed to contribute to accomplishing the HEADER, and to identify which person was to take responsibility for performing the action item. Usually it is a good idea to put a completion date on each SUBBER, but since all the action items were to be done so quickly, dating the action items was not needed.

With the plan now set before us, we began tackling the action items.

First on the agenda was meeting with the staff. We began with Eric Cody, our sales executive/salesman (who was also my son-in-law). We brought him in right away and told him that we were closing the company and that there were to be no further sales put together after 2:00 p.m. the next day. That would allow tucking in an order that was virtually placed but not yet in the system, but would stop any new orders from being generated. We then went over all the orders in the production pipeline and made the determination of how to complete and deliver them. This was important, as we felt that all of the orders in the system could be completed by the end of the month, and we wanted that to be the last payday for our production personnel. After this discussion with Eric, it was agreed that his last day would be the eighteenth.

Then we called a meeting of all of the employees of the company and let them know that the company was going to close down by the end of the month. We let each of them know when we expected their last day to be, as different ones were to be let go sooner than others. We immediately began laying off people that we would not be needing to handle the production of the remaining orders and then followed a structured layoff schedule as the orders were finished up. Everything was designed to keep our payroll expenses down as low as possible and to make sure we had sufficient funds to pay our employees for the work they did.

We did our best to virtually include every aspect of closing down the company in the Storyboard: taking care of our employees and customers, selling the assets, dealing with creditors, and even the cleanup of the building and offices. The Storyboard became our road map, and we left it up on the wall until the whole thing was over. We would go into the conference room, look each item over, check it off, see what was left to be done, revisit things as they were worked, constantly, every day we were there. I can't overemphasize how important this procedure is, not only in creating a business or new idea or concept for a going concern but also in the event one has to be shut down.

If you are interested in more details regarding going through the Headers and Subbers, with the actions taken on them, etc., please visit the **Storyboard Appendix** in the back of the book.

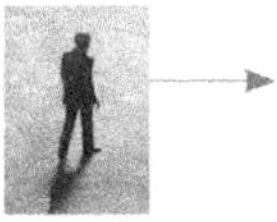

Chapter 9

THE INITIAL STEPS

On the last day of the existence of Phoenix Custom Apparel, we held a company closing party. We brought food in for everyone, gave some memorabilia to those who wanted something to take with them, gave company-manufactured, Phoenix Custom Apparel embroidered jackets to those employees who hadn't yet received one for their five years of service. Attendees shared many a story from the memories of the past nine-and-a-half years, lots of hugs were given to each other, and we finally said our goodbyes through our tears.

Then the smoke and ashes of the Phoenix began to disappear.

Interestingly, one of the two owners of one of our customers had been at the plant when we had the closing party, and I invited him to join us for lunch. We had been doing sublimation printing for them as one of their suppliers, so they often came to the plant to pick up sublimated fabric, and we'd gotten to know each other pretty well. When he asked what was going on and I told him what we were doing, immediately the subject came up regarding what I was going to do with the sublimation equipment. Within minutes, it was agreed that we would put a deal together to sell that equipment to their company and that we would help them put their own sublimation production operation together using our equipment and staff and turn over our sublimation design archives and customer base to them.

With that step, a process I didn't even know existed but would soon learn about, called a "self-managed liquidation," officially began.

The first communication of our decision to close went via a telephone call to our contact person at the National Hot Rod Association. Once again, the window was open there, as we had completed all the orders that NHRA had given us through that decision point in sufficient quantity both as to take care of their needs and to meet our contractual obligations. There was surprise and shock when I told the official of our decision, but it was quick and clean, and we would work with them to assure that the pieces could be reassembled with no harm to them or the racing community.

Once that communication was completed, we went on to our website and posted the closing of Phoenix Custom Apparel right on our Home Page, and let past, present, and future customers know what had been done. We also used the full-page ads we had not yet used for *National Dragster*, the official weekly publication of the NHRA, to announce our closing and to advertise the names and contact information of those who purchased divisions of our company so that past and new customers would know where to go for those products.

Throughout all of our planning, the following things were paramount:

First, complete all the orders in the pipeline and deliver them to our customers, most of whom had either prepaid or made deposits on their orders;

Second, pay all the employees whatever compensation they had coming through the time they worked for the company;

Third, structure the closing in such a manner as to be able to have past customers continue to get the products that they got from us in the past, to make available to them the embroidery digitizing that they had paid for, to make art work accessible for future orders of sublimated products, and to make patterns for firesuits available for future orders; and

Fourth, go through the process of selling off all of the company's assets, funnel that money back to the creditors, and pay them back as much as we possibly could.

It was also imperative, with no income stream to pay monthly payments on debt, that I put a totally new structure together to deal with creditors who were no longer going to be receiving debt-service payments. These debts included working capital and equipment financing for the company, mortgage financing for the real estate owned, and unsecured credit card debt.

Within days of our decision to close, I went down to the Colorado Housing and Finance Authority, who held the first mortgage on our plant, and met with CHFA's Executive Director Roy Alexander. I told him what we had done and why, advised him that we would be unable to continue to make payments on the mortgage, and asked him for a moratorium on those payments until I was able to sell the building and pay off their loan.

I made a similar trip down to Preferred Lending Partners, who managed the SBA second mortgage against our building, and asked for the same moratorium on the monthly payments.

Those moratoriums were granted. We now had created a breather on our largest debt payments.

I then called Paul Kluck, the real estate agent through whom we had purchased the plant back in 2001 and asked if he could meet me at our plant. He came over right away, and I told him we had just made the decision to close the company down and that we needed to put the property on the market right away. We went through the discussion of what the sales price should be and agreed to finalize that as soon as Paul could put a market analysis together to come up with a listing-price recommendation.

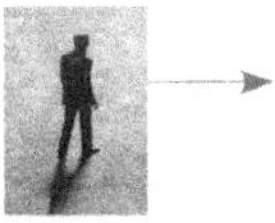

Chapter 10

THE DECISION: Bankruptcy, or Self-Managed Liquidation?

At the end of my conversation with Paul, he suggested that I meet with an acquaintance of his by the name of John Young, who Paul felt was a very good bankruptcy attorney. Following Paul's counsel, I called Mr. Young and had a twenty-five-minute conversation with him. He was encouraging and suggested that we not file bankruptcy but instead do a "self-managed liquidation." He told me, "You're probably not in as bad a shape as you think." He said to keep going forward with my liquidation of assets and dividing up the proceeds to go to the lenders. However, he allowed that he may have a "conflict of interest," as one of my creditors was a client of his and that he would call me back on whether he could represent me or not.

It turned out that he could not represent me, and he recommended that I contact Jeff Brinen of Kutner, Miller and Brinen. So, I did and scheduled a meeting with him for October 19th. I then put together a comprehensive notebook of all of the financial aspects of the company that I could present to him, to help him in giving me advice on what course of action would be best to take.

The notebook included both personal and company financial statements, company sales and profit-and-loss history, with the company debts broken down into unsecured credit card debts, unsecured business loans debts, and secured business debts, with the equipment identified by creditor/loan and real estate debts with the real estate identified. Included in this debt schedule were the lenders, loan numbers, credit line limits, debt balances, monthly payments, interest rates, and maturity dates.

When I met with Jeff, I told him about our company, its history, and what had precipitated our decision to close the business. I told him about the window that I felt was open to us by making the decision we did, and we went carefully through both the company and personal finances. This included going over in detail every debt and all the assets we had accumulated and making some assumptions about what those assets were actually going to bring at market conditions. Those of you who experienced the economy in those days will remember that market conditions were not very bright.

The debt analysis that I had put together showing all the company debt and personal debts my wife and I owed as of August 31, 2009 totaled $1,157,717 with monthly payments of $22,117 for the business debt, and $678,178 with monthly payments of $5,868 for the "personal" debt (a lot of which had come about in my continued attempt to fund our company's losses until we became profitable). The grand total of our debts amounted to $1,835,895, requiring $27,985 per month in payments.

This was pretty daunting, considering neither one of us had gainful employment and were living off our Social Security income.

After we had concluded with the analysis, Jeff said that, in his opinion, I had two options open to me:

Option 1 was to declare bankruptcy and basically just let the courts and the attorneys and the creditors and bankruptcy structure take over and liquidate the assets and pay the creditors off as much as possible. He said that if I took that course of action, I would not have much to do with the process and little, if anything, to say about how things were done, etc. He said that, after the whole process was over and done with, I would be rid of all the assets and liabilities, just walk away clean, and start over. However, our ability to keep our home that we had lived in and raised our family in over the past thirty-eight years—and which had become very dear to us—would be in jeopardy.

Option 2 was to go down the pathway of a "Self-Managed Liquidation." This option would not include any bankruptcy actions and would be totally controlled and managed by me. While it would eliminate the bankruptcy fees for attorney representation and court costs (which would have been substantial, and I had no idea how we would come up with that money), etc., it would require a lot of hard work and negotiation, both in selling the assets and in dealing with and paying off the creditors. He said it would be a difficult process and would require a minimum of one year of my life and quite possibly two. He said that, while this was certainly the harder of the two options, I would have maximum control over how the whole thing was done. He said that, with what I had put together and gone over with him, it looked like there may be enough assets to take care of the creditors with full and/or negotiated, discounted settlements and actually pull the liquidation off successfully, and that once all the debts had been settled, go on from there with my life.

After we kicked the two options around for a brief time, I told Jeff that I wanted to pursue the Self-Managed Liquidation. But I also wanted to retain Jeff as my "Bankruptcy Attorney" to give me counsel and help as I went through the process. He said that was fine with him. He wished me good luck, said that he would be available to help me with anything I needed, and invited me to keep in contact with him as things developed.

And so the die was cast. The process was defined.

I went back to the plant to meet in the conference room with the remaining team and let them know of the decision to do the self-managed liquidation and what that was all about. We then reviewed the Storyboard to see where we were on each of the items on the wall, and, knowing now where we were going and what we faced, we proceeded full steam ahead with that added power of clarity and resolve.

Chapter 11

GOING THROUGH THE GAUNTLET: Part 1 (the easy part)

Selling the Business Assets

September 25, 2009

It is hard to write these words down, as I put myself back into the circumstances that I found myself in on that date. That morning, the plant was buzzing with production activities, getting shipping done, answering phone calls from various parties, etc., the "normal" hubbub of business. Then, when it was all done, and all the orders had been shipped out, and everyone had left, I walked around the nearly twenty thousand square feet of office and manufacturing space with nobody there. There was a deathly quiet throughout the plant. Knowing that no one was coming back, and looking at all of the equipment we had, all the fabric, all the supplies, all the empty desks and chairs and work areas, I wondered: **"WHAT IN THE WORLD AM I GOING TO DO WITH ALL THIS STUFF?!"** Devastating. Sad. Depressing. Scary. Awful. Tearful. And I can feel it now, with all the emotions of that moment. Wow.

Ah, but I was not alone.

I remember one time, when we were going full blast, when I went to a meeting of business owners to talk about common problems we all faced, and the question was asked: "How do you get good employees?" No one had any really good suggestions, and everyone agreed that it was a huge problem. I stood up and told them: "You raise them!" I explained that some of the best employees I ever had were my children, and while that certainly carried its own baggage and trials and tribulations, they were workers you could really depend on to do the job.

And it held true even after the company was closed. My son Matthew, who was our VP of Art/Design, and my daughter Mary, who was our VP of Production, stayed by my side for the next three months to get me through that initial closing process. They helped me in making decisions, in putting together our auction to sell everything inside and outside the plant, in taking care of the auction, in helping in the selling of the "pieces" of the company, in being involved in the structure of those sales, in helping educate and train people on how to use what they bought, and in many, many details that ensued, all of which gave me emotional and mental strength to come in every day and face the tasks at hand. I could never overstate the value and benefit they were in helping me get through this difficult time.

And thus we began the sale of what had constituted Phoenix Custom Apparel.

I had tried to sell the company as a whole but found that was not a viable option, which I discovered fairly early in the process. Just as well. What I found out in "undoing" a company was just the opposite of what you were taught about building companies from the management gurus ("Synergy is the creation of something bigger than the individual parts by combining them together, and is really good to do…"). In our case, what I found out was that the company was more valuable by divesting itself of the individual pieces or departments that had been created in its evolution, and that, by selling each of those pieces off individually, I could get it done quicker for a better settlement structure and price, and could take better care of making sure our past customers had the access to the things that would be of benefit to them in trying to obtain repeat products after we were gone.

As mentioned, the first piece we sold was our Sublimation Division. That went to Craig Pena and Jay Salas, owners of Chingaso and their yet-to-be-formed company called J-C Apparel. Matt worked extensively with me on the valuation of that piece and the structuring of the agreement between our two entities. That even included Matt making his own services as our main graphic artist and technician available to them to give them the foundation of the key art/graphics resource vital to the design and production process. Once the agreement was inked, it didn't take long for them to begin producing quality sublimated products. Matter of fact, it didn't take thirty days. We actually leased some of the space in our plant to them, so they could produce right there in our facility until the end of December, which gave them time to get their own facility prepared for moving the sublimation equipment and setting themselves up in their own plant. Matt and Mary provided constant guidance in how to go about producing sublimated apparel, from art work to file structure to printing to transferring images onto the fabric, and on to the cut-and-sew construction of the finished product. I provided them with a flow structure that we had developed by one of my other children, Scott, who had become our Lean Manufacturing specialist during his time with us, and that flow chart was of great help to Jay and Craig. They took possession of the sublimation equipment, assumed the lease obligation on that equipment, purchased the fabric we had stocked, and were on their way. We were relieved of the most expensive equipment we had acquired and the big debt associated with and secured by that acquisition.

The next piece we sold was the Firesuit Division. Like the Sublimation Division, it went quickly and was sold on the first phone call to the purchaser. Dennis Taylor, owner of Taylor Motorsports Products in Anaheim, California, had come to us when we first started manufacturing firesuits for race car drivers. He was contemplating starting his own firesuit-manufacturing operation. He'd heard of us, and, after a few phone calls (we knew each other pretty well from our times as racing participants on the drag strip, so our trust level was very good), he signed on to become a dealer for Phoenix firesuits. That relationship lasted many years, and we worked closely together during those years to create a top-quality product that was very racer friendly in the features of the suits.

So, I called Dennis and told him we were closing down. I asked if he was now ready to have his own firesuit-manufacturing operation and told him we would sell him our Gerber Technologies CAD CAM pattern-making equipment and software, which also had all the patterns of all the firesuits we had ever made for our customers. We also offered for sale our fire-retardant fabrics that had all been tested in the many tests that we had done with the SFI Foundation, and a new Tajima Single Head Embroidery Machine that was excellent for embroidering the many logos that were embroidered on the firesuits. Included in the offer were the special sewing machines that we used to assemble the suits, complete with the backup and instructions that would be provided to Dennis and his staff by our VP of Production (Mary). It didn't take him long to decide that this was the way for him to go, and our deal was structured within a few weeks. He sent a truck out to pick up the goodies, and, shortly thereafter, Mary and I made a trip to his operation in Anaheim so Mary could give him the final training on all the equipment and processes. Dennis was now in business, producing the same product he had been selling for years.

The third piece of the business was the sale of our Embroidery Division. That went so fast, I couldn't believe it. I really thought that selling the embroidery machines would be the most difficult, and that we would take the biggest hit in what I would get for them, but I was pleasantly wrong. It turned out that our machines were in high demand, and we sold them off to various buyers quickly. The largest acquisition was made by Marty Taylor of Tayco Screen-Printing & Embroidery out of Colorado Springs, Colorado. He was a gem to work with, and, by the time we were done, he had purchased our new 8-Head Tajima, received all of our digitizing files with the express agreement that past customers who had purchased embroidered goods from us would have access to those files, other equipment that was used in the embroidering process, and all of our embroidery thread. That sale also took another good-sized chunk of debt off our plate.

We then used our remaining full-page advertisements in *National Dragster* to let people know that they could go to J-C Apparel for sublimated products that we had previously made for them; to Taylor Motorsports Products for "our" firesuits and to also get their firesuits recertified as needed; and to Tayco Screen-Printing & Embroidery for their embroidery digitizing and be able to get the same embroidered products that they had received from Phoenix.

NHRA had made a deal with a company in California to take over the manufacturing of their Champion Jackets that we had done for years, and with the exception of our "cut and sew" piece (which was really the talented sewers we had on the sew line), we were done selling the company.

With the funds that were generated by the sale of these pieces and the attendant equipment and supply inventories for those specialized divisions, we were able to liquidate the lion's share of our debt structure that related to the business.

But we still had a plant full of furniture, a substantial inventory of fabrics, cutting tables and industrial cutting knives, sewing machines of various types and purposes, electrical tracks to power the sew line, office equipment and supplies, and other equipment used in the manufacturing processes.

So, the question was, "How do we sell off these smaller pieces and all the stuff you accumulate over nearly ten years of business activity?"

Only one answer seemed plausible: **Hold an Auction**.

Well, that's another thing I'd never experienced. How the hell do you do that?!

[As an aside, I must admit here: I was in my element! I was negotiating and putting deals together, taking care of details, trying stuff I had never done before, etc. This was good and exciting and productive. However, it would get worse!]

Back to holding an auction.

What else could I do? I went to that fountain of all wisdom and knowledge: The Internet.

I looked up Auctioneers, and had the good fortune to find a company that, at first glance, looked like a perfect prospect for us: Roller & Associates, Inc.

I found them on the Internet on November 1st. I placed a call at 10:36 a.m. on November 2, and at 11:00 a.m. on November 3, I met with Dayton Roller at our plant to go through the building and all the outstructures to get his thoughts about the advisability and possible success of holding an auction, and see if they were interested in being the auctioneering platform. The walk-through went well, and Dayton said, "We can sell everything! Period." And, he meant *everything*. He recommended that our auction be an "Internet only" auction, and then he took me through how that would work. He shared with me the process of how they would put it all together, beginning with doing a complete inventory identification with photographs that would be published on the Internet, how they would advertise the auction, how things would go on the day of the auction, through to the final settlement, what their fees would be, and when they would be paid. On November 13, I was given the proposed contract for the auction. On November 19, I faxed the executed contract to Kurk Near, who was the responsible party for our auction, and the auction was set for December 17, 2009.

Wow. What a process. These people have it all down to a science. Thank goodness for Matt and Mary, again, who watched over everything, helped organize things in convenient groupings, answered questions on equipment and how it was used, and backed up all of our computers and cleaned off all of the hard drives, etc, etc, etc. Together, we worked closely with Kurk and his crew, and on December 16, we were present to be available for questions from prospective purchasers who came into the plant to look over the auction items during our pre-auction preview. Then, on the seventeenth, we sat at our computers and watched as the bidding took place.

What a trip!

By the end of the day, everything was auctioned off except eight old, beat-up desks and four old, beat-up credenzas. I was totally amazed, and very pleased at the results—both getting rid of everything *and* the amount of money we realized from the auction.

By the following Tuesday, December 22, pretty much everything that had been purchased was gone, and the few items that remained were there by agreement with the purchasers who came and picked them up within a few days. By January 7, 2010, all sales were accounted for in a final statement from Roller, and we received the check for the net proceeds.

I now had a building that was empty, except for some old furniture I kept in my office to be able to do work in the building until it was sold and the few pieces that hadn't been auctioned off. I could now begin the process of cleaning up, painting up, and fixing up to make the building more presentable to prospects.

In all, within three months of closing down the company, I had an empty building.

I still went to the plant every day. My work there was continuing the process of negotiating the payoff of the remaining debts, working with Paul on showing the building to prospects, and physically taking care of the property.

By this time, the company debt structure had been reduced by $349,891 (which amounted to 61 percent of the non-real-estate debt), with monthly payments lowered by $9,141 per month (which amounted to 72 percent of the non-real-estate payments).

Keep in mind that, while we were selling all of the company assets, my wife and I were also selling personal assets, including other real estate we had accumulated over the years, all with the purpose of getting that debt load reduced.

During these three months, some things started to rear their ugly heads that gave some indication that the road ahead was going to get much more difficult. Nothing could have been more accurate.

Chapter 12

GOING THROUGH THE GAUNTLET: Part 2 (the hard part)

Paying off the Real Estate Debt

Back in the summer of 1981, when I was installed as the president of the Colorado Mortgage Lenders Association at our annual convention up in Vail, interest rates were at their all-time high, and all of us mortgage bankers were totally sucking wind. The keynote speaker to open the convention was a bond trader for Merrill Lynch out of New York City, and in his opening remarks to an audience that was literally sitting on the edge of their seats, hoping to hear this out-of-town expert tell us that interest rates were going to start coming down, the sky would be clearing, and good times were in the foreseeable future, he began his remarks by stating:

"Just remember: It always gets darkest just before it gets pitch black."

You can imagine our dismay at hearing those words. And, unfortunately, his statement turned out to be a very accurate prediction of what was to come. Things got way worse before they got better.

To give you an idea of just how high rates got in that time period, the Prime Rate that banks used as their foundation rate got to 22 percent, and the rate on a new FHA-insured, thirty-year mortgage reached 17.5 percent.

I can say that, once again, I was about to experience our Merrill Lynch bond trader's prophetic statement, albeit in another venue.

Time to fasten your seat belt.

Meetings With My Two Real Estate Lenders

With my background in mortgage banking, I knew that it was imperative that I have a discussion with the two real estate lenders that held the first and second mortgages on our "plant," which consisted of a twenty-thousand-square-foot office/warehouse building on a one and one-half-acre plot of ground in the North Denver area. To purchase the property on December 5, 2001, I had negotiated the first mortgage as a purchase-money mortgage with the Colorado Housing and Finance Authority (CHFA) for $500,000. I also assumed the existing second mortgage that was an SBA "504" loan, which was being managed by the Denver Urban Economic Development Corporation (later known as Preferred Lending Partners) here in Denver. At the time of the purchase of the property, that loan amounted to $285,000. My wife and I paid the difference between the loans and the sales price in cash at the closing table.

Since the source of making the monthly payments to these two lenders was the business I had just decided to close, I immediately contacted Roy Alexander, the Executive Director of CHFA, to set up a meeting. I met with him on September 23, 2009. I told him of our decision to close the company down and that I wanted to work with CHFA on keeping things steady as we went down the road with no income to make the payments. I asked him to see if CHFA could give me a moratorium on making the monthly payments until I could get the property sold and pay their loan off.

The next day, September 24, I had contact with Stephanie Gerringer, Executive Director of Preferred Lending Partners, and Megan Melich, their Portfolio Manager, and had a similar discussion with them.

The initial contacts with these lenders were positive in terms of notifying them of the problem and beginning to work out steps to keep things right side up and preventing a foreclosure situation, with the intent always being to pay everyone off in full, one way or another. Ultimately, I received a moratorium on monthly payments from both lenders for a time period that would, hopefully, get us through a sale and closing.

Preferred Lending Partners and their staff were absolutely awesome to work with from the get-go. I could not have hoped for a more sympathetic and supportive team and organization to work with than them. And, that continued from beginning to end.

CHFA, however, was a whole other ball game. Wow. What a meat grinder. Interestingly, I had been on the board of directors of CHFA from February 9, 1984 through July 17, 1997, and, during those nearly fourteen years, served for one year as Chairman of the Board. What that meant regarding this transaction was that I knew my way around the loan programs that CHFA offered the public, and I knew the players. But, I never asked for, received, or expected any kind of treatment that would be different from any other applicant/customer that came through CHFA's doors. That was a given. However, I was not prepared for the way I was treated once Roy (whom I had known for many years from my time on the board) turned me over to a member of their Commercial Workout staff. From the very beginning, I had the impression from the person I was assigned to that she did not think very highly of me for having the financial problems that kept me from making the monthly payments on their loan and putting the loan into a default status. And because of the way she conducted our interactions that feeling never went away.

I invited both Megan Melich and CHFA's representative to come visit with me at the property, so that I could show them through the building and the grounds, and discuss what our plans were. Megan was out to our building in days; it took CHFA until the 19th of October to set foot in our building. Megan was right there with me in where we were heading. The day after the CHFA representative met with me at the building, however, I was on the phone to Roy to tell him I really needed someone who could understand what was going on and would work with me on getting everything resolved. Unfortunately, Roy then left CHFA, and it took a while for CHFA to come up with Roy's replacement. Once that took place, I set up a personal visit to the new Executive Director, with whom I was acquainted, and asked for and was granted my request to work with other people within the CHFA organization, who were very supportive and helpful throughout the process. At the end of the day, however, I guess organizational structure trumped arrangements, and the final six months of this twenty-two-month ordeal were brutal, as my former workout specialist once again became my taskmaster.

Throughout it all, however, this proactive stance on my part in working with CHFA and PLP did work well for all parties.

Bless their hearts, PLP and the SBA continued to work with us and kept us in a payment-deferred status up until we closed on the sale of our building. What a help that was, in every respect.

However, in the wisdom of my workout specialist and CHFA, a Notice of Election and Demand (in other words, the initiation of foreclosure proceedings) was filed on March 8, 2011. The foreclosure sale date, at which the property would be sold at public auction through the Public Trustee's Office in downtown Denver, was set for July 7, 2011.

The race was on.

Getting the Property on the Market

It was time to get the plant listed and on the market.

Once the decision was made to close the company, in the midst of selling off all the company assets, I also began the process of finding a buyer for the real estate. I immediately talked to my next-door neighbor to the west, Gourmet Fine Catering. Over time, I had gotten pretty close with Kent Kidwell, the general manager and one of the owners of Gourmet. Kent said there was an interest in our building and that he would begin exploring that possibility. I never could get in touch with my neighbor to the east, and as they had just purchased their property within the past year or so and had poured a ton of money into remodeling the entire structure, that did not seem like it would be a fruitful path to pursue.

Paul Kluck put an analysis of recent sales and current listing data together, and we met to go over that information and determine a listing price. Interestingly, he said that there was a demarcation line that showed a distinctly different market from one side of that line to the other. The dividing line date was October of 2008—which just happened to be the month immediately after the fall of Lehman Brothers, which I have already spoken of earlier in this book as the defining event leading to the collapse of the U.S. economy. Anyway, Paul had comparable sales data for pre-October 2008 and post-October 2008, plus the twenty-one current listings of properties near our plant.

In the end, we decided on a listing price of $900,000 ($125,000 less than we had bought the property for in 2000 and significantly down from the $1,200,000 value of just a few years earlier). I signed an Exclusive Right-to-Sell Listing Contract with Paul and his company CB Richard Ellis on November 3, 2009. Paul put a large CBRE For Sale sign over our Phoenix Custom Apparel sign in the front of the building, and we were officially on the market.

The Deals

From the very beginning, it seemed like Paul and I had an ideal structure for a quick sale: He was out doing his thing in the market place, sending off e-mails to all the active commercial real estate brokers, contacting his own clients, fielding calls, and following up on leads, etc., and I was in the building every day doing my own work on the self-managed liquidation process and thus was available to visit and conduct a tour of the property with anyone who happened to drive by the property and see the For Sale sign up in the front. I am also a licensed real estate broker, so I knew how to handle real estate transactions professionally.

Deals started coming our way, and some were way more interesting than others. Here are a few that we worked on:

- The first serious bite was from the leadership of the Iglesia De Jesucristo. They felt the building was perfect for their needs as a larger facility for their Church, and that the large lot gave them ample parking for their congregation. Paul put a Letter of Intent to Purchase together, which they signed at full price on December 21, 2009. They were so enthused about the property and so energetic about every aspect of putting this deal together, that I allowed them to "rent" the property for a New Year's Celebration Dinner that was to be held on December 31st, and two other Sunday meetings, so their congregation could get a feel for how the building would work out for them. Money changed hands, and then they came in and built a stage in the warehouse area where our manufacturing had taken place, for their musicians to use in their meetings. They had many meetings, and Julie and I and some of our family even attended one of their Sunday-night services, just to see what they were all about. They were great people, and it really looked like the property would work well for them, but, unfortunately, in the end, they couldn't raise the money to purchase the property, and the deal died. That was sad for all.

- Near the end of January 2010, a well-dressed young man came into the building and asked me if I could take him through the place. He was interested in the property becoming what he called his "Medical Marijuana Mall," and, after the tour, he was very excited about the possibilities, as he felt the property was perfect for what he had in mind. I did an unbelievable amount of work with this person, through a number of months. I, too, felt that he had a great idea and that the concept could really be a leader in the newly passed Medical Marijuana law in the State of Colorado. It could be a real benefit to the industry developing properly and in the customers that the mall would be serving. In the end, however, it turned out that the young man could not produce the financial support that he thought he could, and being unable to come up with funding required to buy the property, that deal went south. Interestingly enough, there were many more attempts of the MMJ community to purchase the property, but nobody could come up with the cash or financing to complete a transaction.
- In July, we got an offer for $850,000 from a window manufacturer that went to Contract and called for the assumption of both the CHFA first mortgage and the SBA second mortgage. In the end, we were able to get approval from the SBA of the assumption of the second but, to our dismay, CHFA rejected the assumption of their loan by this purchaser. In spite of our attempts to resurrect a sale

involving other financing, the deal cratered. That was a serious bummer that hurt everyone.

- During this first nine months after listing the property, we seemed to have a nonending supply of interested parties in the property. I hammered out deals; Paul brought in deals; live deals like the Church and the window manufacturer couldn't get to home plate. The number of offers started to dwindle pretty drastically. So I started looking at any way I could either lease the building with sufficient income stream to pay the monthly payments on the existing loans and just ride it out, or anything else that I could conceive, even if it didn't make sense.
- One of those desperate attempts at making the property an income producer was to turn it into an Event Center. Through my Gourmet contacts, I had a lady who wanted to lease the property for a one-day event. Well, why not?! So, I put the deal together and got the building all spruced up and opened it up for their lighting people, their sound people, the tables and chairs, etc., etc., etc., all for putting on a one-night blast for their guests. The Holiday Event was to be held on Saturday night, December 4, 2010. It actually went very well, and the building and lot area were perfect for what they staged. With that encouragement, I began working with Gourmet's owners to put a Joint Venture together that could generate activities and events that would make the operation profitable and generate enough income to cover our mortgage debts, etc. and actually turn a profit. I did number-crunching, created spreadsheets galore, put agreement after agreement together, and had meeting after

meeting, but I just couldn't get it done. Sometime in January or February of 2011, I finally gave up the ghost and let it die a natural death.

Meantime, while all this was going on, in its own special brand of wisdom, the City and County of Denver's Assessor decided that the Actual Valuation of our property needed to go up by 31 percent, raising our taxes by 28 percent. Have you folks checked the real estate market lately? At a time when we were unable to be making our mortgage payments, our delinquency amount was now going up even faster. My letter of protest to the Board of Equalization sent on January 22, 2010 went unanswered. Surprise.

During all this time, as I worked diligently to clean up the building and have it in shape for showings and events, etc., the one activity that brought great personal stress relief was when, sometime after the auction was done and the Church had finally moved their stuff out of the building, I had these eight desks and four credenzas that never sold and were in such condition that nobody would want or could even use them. So, I asked Mary's husband if he had a large sledgehammer. He said he had a twenty-pound one with a long handle that he would be happy to lend me. I took it, and went back into the warehouse area, where I'd moved all that junk, and instead of taking a screw driver and disassembling everything, I put myself near the center of the warehouse area and took my first swing at a desk. Man, you should have heard the noise and seen the stuff flying everywhere. I found out that, with some well-directed blows with a long-handled, twenty-pound sledgehammer, you can disassemble the most formidable desk or credenza in about sixty seconds, and that, even better, the resulting pieces are so small that you can toss them into a dumpster without any problem whatsoever. And the best thing was the thoughts you can let go through your mind when you are swinging that sledge. Talk about therapy. Absolutely awesome! The only bad part about that experience was that I ran out of stuff I could demolish way too quickly.

And You Thought It Couldn't Get Worse

I continued to occupy the building until April of 2010, when I underwent my second full knee-replacement surgery. At that point, my children decided that it was time for me to vacate the property and get away from the burdens and pressures that being there every day subjected me to, so they came in and pretty much emptied my office and moved me back into our home.

I still went up to the property two or three times a week, and worked constantly on getting the small details cleaned up, fixed up, etc., to make the property look better for a sale. I continued to work on deals and work with Paul, so things were still going forward with as much energy as before to get the property sold.

It was now Friday, December 31, 2010. New Year's Eve day. The gateway to a year of dealing with all the remaining creditors who hadn't yet been paid off, and pushing that string of selling the building, and of working every thought and angle that I could come up with to get things back right-side-up.

At 2:48 p.m., I received the following e-mail from my friend Kent Kidwell from Gourmet Fine Catering, my next-door neighbor:

"Hey, Bruce—my power just got restored at GFC. Waste Management knocked over the power pole this a.m. Your building is without power. I don't have your cell number, or I would have called sooner."

Really?

The weather for several weeks had been in the zero-degrees area, some nights above and some below zero, with no end in sight. With no electricity, we had no heat. With no heat, you can guess what was going to happen to every water pipe in the building and what that would do to it. We had a full, overhead, fire sprinkling system in the entire warehouse area. What a mess that could become, let alone all the other water lines throughout the building to service bathrooms, etc.

I immediately began making phone calls to Xcel Energy to find out if our power was also going to be restored that day, like it had been at Gourmet. I hadn't even had a chance yet to drive up to the building. I was just trying to get as much handled from a phone call, as quickly as possible. Dan from Xcel advised me, "You need to get an electrician to reinstall everything" .... "for us to hook up the electricity." He said that the electrical conduit box and pipes and wiring were torn down off the building, and they could not restore power until everything was put back together.

Oh, no. I immediately got on my horse and headed up to the plant to see for myself what had happened.

What a disaster.

I found Kent, and together we looked the situation over. Kent told me that when Waste Management's dump truck was picking up their trash that morning, on the way out, they managed to hook the guy wire holding up the power pole—and actually pulled the power pole down, transformer and all. Somehow the wiring on Gourmet's building did not get ripped off, but it sure did on mine. When Xcel Energy got out there, they restored Gourmet's electricity, but they cut my wires from the power source because there was no way they could fix my problem.

And it was *cold!* Right at two degrees above zero. I later printed out the National Weather Service temperature history for the first part of January, and on January 1, 2011, the high was nineteen degrees, and the low was two degrees.

It was also New Year's Eve! And, right at 5:00 p.m. Time to get things moving.

I needed to get the water drained out of every pipe and system I could. This included the office areas with bathrooms up in the front seven thousand square feet of the building, and the bathrooms and overhead fire sprinkling system and water supply and backflow prevention systems in the thirteen-thousand-square-foot manufacturing area. And, while I know how to drain a pipe, I had no idea how to drain a commercial sprinkling system and some of the other systems.

Thankfully, a very dear friend of mine and drag-racing buddy by the name of John Abbott had a company called Fire & Safety, who I'd had install and service my fire extinguishers throughout the building over the years. I called John, told him what had transpired, and asked if there was any way he could locate someone to come to the building—*now*—and help me drain the building. He found someone who was up in the mountains skiing at Keystone who was willing to come down and work with me. I began draining what I could find and do by myself, and about seven o'clock pm, my helper showed up; we began draining the fire sprinkling system. Then, we drained the hot-water heater, opened up all the valves we could find, and got our emergency winterizing taken care of. I was without lights (something I forgot about on the way up to the building), and Kent let me borrow a bunch of great work flashlights that we used to get things drained. We finally left the plant at nine thirty p.m., frozen—but with the systems drained.

At five o'clock am the next morning, I woke up worrying about the need to shut down the entire water supply to the building from the main water supply out in the street. So, I called Denver Water, and they thought we should do that. So, back up I went, and at 6:45 a.m., we got that shut down, too.

Damage control was now completed. Happy New Year!

Then began the process of dealing with Waste Management. Truthfully, while it started out pretty typical, dealing with a large company who neither knew nor cared about Bruce Bowler or Phoenix Custom Apparel or 3660 E. 40th Avenue, I was able to talk to enough of the right people who got me to the really right people who could, and did, step up to the plate and worked with me on getting our building repaired. They turned out to be honorable in their dealings and funded the reconstruction costs appropriately.

I now became the general contractor in charge of repairing the building and getting all systems back up and running.

Somehow I got in contact with a company by the name of Ideal Electric, who came out and gave me a bid on January 14th. I awarded them the contract, and they set about getting the electrical system restored. I had to hire a concrete man to put in a new concrete pad for the electrical system, which got done in time for Ideal Electric to complete their work. I hired a plumber to restore the water system, brought back Fire & Safety to restore the fire sprinkling system, and got the final numbers together and sent off to Waste Management.

By the end of February, we had the electrical system all repaired, compliments of funding from Waste Management. I temporarily held off on getting water back into the building so that we didn't have to pay heat bills while selling the building. By May, when the weather was friendly, all systems were up and running, and the repairs were complete.

We're Under Contract!

In the midst of all the reconstruction and dealing with the legalities of the foreclosure action of CHFA, the sales effort never missed a beat.

And, lo and behold, on April 22, 2011, we had a bona fide CONTRACT TO BUY AND SELL REAL ESTATE offer on the table for a price of $798,000. The price hurt some, but it was a real deal and would pay off the two mortgage loans in full. On April 25, 2011, I accepted the offer, and we were under contract. Under the terms of the Contract, the closing date was to take place sixty-five days after the date of acceptance, which put it on Wednesday, June 29, 2011.

The foreclosure sale was scheduled for Thursday, July 7, some four business days after the scheduled closing date.

The race really was on now.

Getting from Contract to Closing in any real estate transaction is almost never easy. That's why there are real estate agents, specialists in not only putting together transactions but, more importantly, *keeping* them together and dealing with the myriad of issues that pop up along the way such that the transaction actually makes it to the closing table. I won't take you through all the details of our sixty-five-day road trip, but there were a few notable bumps in the road that we had to deal with that I will mention here, just so you don't think this was a piece of cake.

- The first item of business was, now that we had a buyer, we needed to get the electricity turned back on and the water and fire sprinkler systems back fully restored and operative. I began the systematic process of getting all those systems operational. In the end, we had to replace a backflow-prevention device, repair one broken pipe in a ceiling in one of the front offices, and get the polarization of the electrical system reversed on the day of the closing, but that was it. All the repairs worked fine and were able to be checked out to the purchaser's satisfaction.

- Now enters the difficulty in paying your lender off. I never had one issue or problem with Preferred Lending Partners and the Small Business Administration. They were straight up and very helpful every step of the way. However,

Colorado Housing and Finance Authority, the lender on whose board of directors I'd served for fourteen years, was totally the opposite, and that was the case down to the very end in giving us a Payoff Statement. The Payoff Statement is the document that shows the Title Company just how much money has to be paid to the lender in order to get a Release of Deed of Trust (the mortgage) from them.

A little history here to help understand this piece:

Back on Friday, March 11, 2011, I was contacted by some parties interested in purchasing our property, and they said that they needed the absolute best price I could offer them in exchange for a quick closing. I immediately contacted CHFA and Preferred Lending Partners to get Payoff Statements. At 4:40 p.m., I received a payoff amount from CHFA of $452,866.46, which was the amount to pay off their loan as of March 31, 2011. Perfect. I also got a figure from Preferred Lending, and I was off and running. I put a Contract together that night and met with the prospective buyer the next morning to go over the Contract. Everything was agreed to, with the only caveat being that the property needed to meet certain zoning requirements for the buyer, but that if it did, we had a deal.

Lucky I hadn't signed that Contract, because on Monday, March 14, I received an e-mail from CHFA stating that they had made an error in calculating the payoff amount and that the new number was $467,255.92! A $14,000 increase in the payoff amount. If I had signed the Contract, that money would have had to come out of my pocket at the closing table.

As it turned out, the zoning turned out not to be satisfactory to the buyer, so they walked. We were actually lucky on this one.

Then came the April 22nd Contract, and we were now on our way to the closing table. On June 8, I received a written Payoff Statement from my reassigned CHFA workout specialist via an e-mail, based upon the stipulated closing date of June 29th. That payoff amount was $478,764.62. *Ouch!* This keeps getting higher and higher, way more, it seemed, than what just accrued interest would justify. Oh, well. Let's close.

Then, I got one more e-mail from that individual at 11:00 a.m. on Monday, June 27, two days prior to the closing date with the question: "Do you require an updated payoff?" When I responded that the current Payoff Statement I had was satisfactory, she came back and asked for the information on who to contact at the Title Company and that she would "provide an updated payoff directly to the title company." I knew I was in trouble again. Sure enough, a *revised* Payoff Statement was, in fact, given to the Title Company, some twenty-six hours and seventeen minutes before closing, increasing the payoff amount by an additional $659.87.

I thought it was interesting when the Title Company e-mailed CHFA with the following request: "Please confirm that CHFA is irrevocably / unconditionally committed to releasing lien of record upon receipt of payoff funds." This is not a common request, as title companies pretty much take what they get from a lender as gospel and proceed accordingly. Apparently this Title Company wasn't in a trusting mood with CHFA, either. It only made sense to ask for that confirmation, after all the changes we had been given.

- Our closing was scheduled for Thursday, the 29th. On Thursday, June 23, Paul Kluck contacted me, advising that we had a problem. The purchaser had a sewer-line inspection done; he had received a report that the sewer main needed replacing and that the cost was going to be $64,400. The purchaser was willing to split the difference but wanted us to give them a credit of $32,200 off the sale price at the closing table.

  Well, there goes the sale. We did not have room in the transaction for a $32,200 credit and certainly didn't have that kind of money in our own pockets.

  So, I got on the phone to a company my wife and I had used to do some sewer-line repairs in our home, and I met him up at the property the next day. He took his camera and ran it from the bathroom all the way out the building and clear up to where the sewer main met with the main City line in the street. His camera showed that the sewer main from the building to the street was in fine condition. He did find that there was a collapsed sewer line where the line ran underneath the building on the east side and that it was causing the back-up problems we had experienced before. He said that he would charge us $3,750 to replace the broken section and could have it done in one day.

  I relayed that information back to the purchaser, along with a copy of the DVD sewer line camera scope that my contractor had made. He asked to meet my guy up at the plant and go over everything, which was readily agreed to, and the meeting was set up for 1:00 p.m. on Friday, June 24th.

After that meeting was completed, I talked to the purchaser and told him that, in the interests of bringing this transaction to the closing table on the scheduled date, I would agree to giving him a credit of $10,000 against the purchase price. After due consideration, the purchaser accepted my offer, and we were off to the closing.

▪ So it was that we were all there at the closing table in the offices of Fidelity National Title Insurance Company, and all the documents got signed, and it was all *done*.

Oops.

▪ Except for one significant detail: The money from the purchaser's lender hadn't come in to the Title Company yet, *and they could not disburse*. That meant that not only did I not get our measly Net Proceeds from the sale but also, even more importantly, that neither CHFA nor the SBA were going to get their loans paid off. What!!! I have only four more days left before this property goes on the auction block!

Well, the Title Company closer said they would contact the lender and find out where the wire transfer was and not to sweat it—they would get it all taken care of ASAP. So, Paul, picking up on where I was headed mentally and physically, grabbed me and said to go with him, as he was going to take me to lunch while they mucked through all that. I said "OK," and we walked over to a really nice restaurant. I got settled down, and Paul treated me to a very tasty meal. The good news is that while we were still there, Paul got a text message to come back to the Title Company: The funds were in, all the checks had been written, and the wires to pay off the loans had all been sent. We were *closed!!!*

What a relief I felt, and what gratitude came over me.

Paul and I went back to the Title Company. Paul got his commission check, and I got our Net Proceeds check for $15,894.69. Paul and I shook hands, hugged, and were off to the next of life's challenges.

- One very memorable thing at the closing that I want to mention: Stephanie Geringer, the head of Preferred Lending Partners, attended the closing, which I thought was really great. Then, when I was leaving, she got up out of her chair, met me outside the conference room where the closing had taken place, gave me a hug, and said nice things about working with me and that she was so happy we were able to bring this to a good conclusion. Tearfully, I thanked her for all she had done for us. What a sweet moment that was. Thank you, Stephanie!

[illegible] me a [illegible] and Paul handed me a [illegible] while we were [illegible] Paul got [illegible] someone back to the [illegible] The [illegible] all the checks had been [illegible] to pass [illegible] the [illegible]

When [illegible] over me.

Paul and I [illegible] had put a [illegible] and [illegible] to the [illegible]

One year [illegible] thing that I want [illegible] phone [illegible] head of [illegible] she got up [illegible] the conference room [illegible] and said [illegible] she was [illegible] conclusion [illegible] When [illegible]

Chapter 13

GOING THROUGH THE GAUNTLET: Part 3 (the *really* hard part)

Paying off the Unsecured Debt

As I was going over my book, reviewing everything and making the last-minute revisions, I realized that I had neglected to insert one of the most important segments of all: The trials and tribulations and keys of negotiating the settlement of the unsecured debts.

Just to make it clear, the "secured" debt, like debt that was incurred in the financing of big-ticket equipment to do our business, like $60,000 embroidery machines and $100,000 sublimation equipment, all got taken care of in one way or another when that equipment got sold, so it is not included here. When we sold off the three major segments of the company, those debts got paid off.

I think I "missed" this segment because it was probably the most difficult, and a very painful, part of this whole process.

Taking care of the real estate side of things was pretty dicey, as you have read, but a lot of that is technical, straightforward things to address and take care of. It was difficult at times, for sure, but at least I was generally pretty clear on what needed to be done and how to get to the conclusion.

Way not so when you are short of the funds needed to pay off your unsecured creditors. And that was where we were finding ourselves.

Keep in mind that, while we were selling all of the company assets, my wife and I were also selling personal assets, including other real estate we had accumulated over the years, all being sold to get that debt load settled. You'll read about that in the next chapter, but it's time I went through the grueling experience of dealing with unsecured creditors, like credit-card companies and banks who provided working capital lines of credit.

Here I will give you one of the *big* keys to getting through this mess. Understand that we had no income available to make payments on this unsecured debt, which amounted to about $400,000, with payment obligations of more than $7,000 per month.

Also understand that I went into this thinking, *How hard can this be?* since I had been in mortgage lending most of my adult life dealing with debt, etc. I thought, *I'll just call up each of these unsecured creditors and tell them what happened and that I lost millions of dollars trying to build and keep a business going, and just negotiate some sort of final settlement for so many cents on the dollar, and get it done.*

Here came a big dose of reality therapy. Every person I talked to with that introduction to the conversation told me, "Well, Mr.

Bowler, the problem is that you are current on your monthly payments, so we can't even talk about a settlement."

"But, I just told you I am no longer going to make the monthly payments on my debt to you, and I would like to negotiate a settlement."

"What do you not understand when I told you that, as long as you remain current (which, by the way, I found means being a lot more than just one month delinquent), we cannot discuss a settlement?"

Wow. That's the real world.

"So, you're telling me that I need to stop making the monthly payments on all these debts. Then I have to put up with getting the incessant phone calls from each of you creditors asking where my monthly payment is and when am I going to be able to bring the debt current. Then, I keep on telling you the same story that I told you during the first debt-collection phone call—which I know you entered into some sort of computer system for your records but still insist on getting a repeat of every time we have a conversation. Then I have to hope that, at some point in time before my financial world (and my mind) totally blows to kingdom come, we might be able to have a discussion on arriving at some number that I can miraculously come up with to settle the debt and get it off my obligations?"

"Yes."

It didn't take long (sometimes I am a quick learner) to realize that I had to make some mental adjustments in what I was facing and going to go through to be able to keep my sanity.

So here's what I came to realize. It's what I call one of the "keys" to going through negotiating with unsecured creditors, and it became my foundation, my mantra, my rock that absolutely allowed me to get to the end:

This is a *game*.

That's it!

They are unquestionably playing a game. I had to buy into the concept and the reality that this was a game, and make a statement to myself and the world that I was ready, willing, and able to play the game.

One quick example: During the time that we were getting constant, invasive, frequent phone calls from all the creditors that we were not making payments to, you start to get to know some of them, as they had been "assigned" to your case. After many calls from a man who had come to kind of know me, and knew my history, and what I had gone through, and was now experiencing, as we were going through the rhetoric one evening, he, with some real empathy in his voice, stated to me, "When you get collection calls, you probably know from the phone number that comes up on your phone screen who it is—right?" I said, "Yes, that's true." He then said, "Just don't answer it!" He further said to answer them once in a while, just to keep the lines of communication open, and let them know that I wasn't trying to run and hide. But, not all the time. He was encouraging me, even teaching me, how to play the game. I thought, *That's awesome. Done deal.*

Game on!!!

When I was going through all my gyrations with my real estate activities, I found that I had to get into my "fighting mode" to deal with all that I was encountering. This was different. An entirely different mind-set was being required. I still needed to be in that fighting mode to confront what I had to confront with the unsecured lenders, but I could never lose sight of the fact that I was *playing a game.*

So let's see how that game is played.

When I first visited with my bankruptcy attorney, Jeff identified some of the debts that he felt we were not personally obligated for and suggested that we just tell them to go away. In some cases, that worked out; in others, it didn't. But, it was a good start in separating debtors out based upon having personal liability for the debt or not, and further helping me set the stage for how I was going to play the game with each of them.

Let's start out with Capital One.

A few years before I closed the company down, I got a phone call one day at the office from Capital One and was told that our company was eligible for an unsecured working capital loan of $99,999. I said, "Really—what do I have to do to obtain that funding?"

The gentleman said, "Just answer a few questions about the length of time your company has been in business and the annual volume of business you have."

I said, "Ask away!" and thus I was asked a few simple questions that I readily provided the answers to. He spent a few minutes on his computer most likely running credit reports and whatever else he needed to do to come to a decision, and then told me that Phoenix Custom Apparel had qualified for the loan.

Cool. What do I have to do to get the money?

He said a check for the $99,999 would be coming to us in the mail, made out to Phoenix Custom Apparel, and all I had to do was to deposit it into our company bank account and start using the money.

I asked if I needed to submit some sort of loan application or if I would get a promissory note to sign, or anything like that. He said, "No, just deposit the check." I asked what the interest rate was and what the monthly payment would be, and how I would know what to pay and where. He gave me the information I asked for and said not to worry—a monthly statement would come every month and that I was just to pay from that statement.

"Well, then, send the check." He said, "OK," and our conversation was over.

About an hour later, I went to a business luncheon, where I sat at a table with two owners of a Credit Bureau and told them I just made the smartest or the dumbest move of my life. I told them about the phone conversation and about the information I gave to the caller, and that he said I was approved for this unsecured loan and would be getting a check in the mail. I told them either I was about to be taken for a ride because of the information I had divulged, or I was going to get the easiest loan ever known to mankind.

Well, within the week, the check arrived, made out to the company for the amount stated. I immediately took it down to my bank and deposited it into my account. I did not endorse the back of the check in any way. I just let my bank do their normal stamp on the back that showed it was to be deposited to our bank account. Then I waited to see if, in fact, the funds would show up in the bank account. Lo and behold, in a few days, the funds were there in my account, all ready to be used as I saw fit.

Those were the good old days of lending, for sure, when the banking institutions were doing everything they could to get you to borrow money from them.

I made those payments faithfully, and on time, from the very first payment due until the day I stopped making payments in October of 2009.

By the time I had stopped making the payments, the loan balance had dropped down to $67,301. This was one loan that Jeff was adamant about that we had no personal liability for and thus was not going to require any payment from my wife and me whatsoever. It was a business loan to a Colorado corporation, and the business was gone. Sorry 'bout that. We lost millions, you lose $67,000.

So, that was the posture I took with Capital One from the get-go when the game started. I was cordial when they made their collection calls, told them what had happened, and explained that since there was no loan application I had made, no application I had signed, no promissory note that I had executed, no nothing except a deposited check that was mailed to me as the result of a phone call, I told them that I'd been advised by my attorney that I had no personal liability for the loan, and that I was not going to pay anything further on the debt.

Well, as you can imagine, that didn't set well. And, you would be right.

Once I was asked if I had a bankruptcy attorney. I said, "Yes, and my bankruptcy attorney said that he would be happy to talk with you if you'd just call him."

Then came, "Well, have you filed for bankruptcy?"

"No."

"Then I can't call your attorney."

"Why?"

"Because you haven't filed for bankruptcy."

Surprise. So, the game continued.

Over the months, I kept telling the same story to people who got higher and higher up the ladder, at increasing levels of intensity and decreasing levels of cordiality, until the calls finally stopped. For a time. Then, around the end of February, I got a phone call from a gentleman with a company called Coface North America. It seems that how the system really works is that, once you quit making your payments for so many months, the creditor finally gives up and sends your debt to a collection agency. My research would indicate that perhaps they sell those loans for pennies on the dollar to these companies, who then use their own special tactics to get funds out of the debtor, and, depending upon how much it gets settled for, they make a profit on their investment.

Or, maybe it's just a separate department of the creditor with a different name. I don't really know.

Regardless of what the real situation was, I patiently told the man from Coface what had transpired. Interestingly, during our conversation I discovered that he was a person who understood the losses that my wife and I had suffered in our business venture, and actually gave some recognition of what we had and were going through. But, nevertheless, he said, we still had this debt that really needed to be taken care of.

When I told him the story of how the funds came to be in my bank account, his reaction was one of total disbelief—that it just *could not be* that there was no documentation surrounding this debt. He said he would do his research, come up with the loan documents, and be getting back to me. "Fine," I said. "I'll look forward to your return call."

A couple of weeks went by, and I wondered if I'd ever hear from him again. Then the phone rang, and there he was. He said he had done his research, gone into the archives, and found out that I was absolutely correct. There was no documentation on the loan whatsoever. He complimented me for making the payments on time, until I stopped making them, and then asked if I would like to negotiate a settlement.

Wahoo!! I had finally gotten to the point of negotiating a settlement with an unsecured lender.

In our ensuing discussion, the fact that my attorney told me I had no obligation to pay anything to anybody to settle this account was acknowledged. But this man also said that it may be in our best interests to settle the account, inasmuch as it would show up on our credit report that the debt had been "settled" rather than "written off." I understood the wisdom in that concept and asked just what he had in mind as a settlement amount. He said if I could see my way clear to paying 10 percent of the amount of the debt (which, by now, was at $69,097) and make a payment to them of $7,000, I would be given a letter that this account had been settled in full.

I had him get that offer to me in writing, reviewed it with my attorney, signed it, found the $7,000 to get to him, and this debt was settled.

We were on our way. This really *was* a *game!*

Enjoy this moment, Bruce. It's going to get tougher as we go along.

Speaking of sweet moments, as a brief digression, let me take this opportunity to give you another secret, or key, that I learned while going through the gauntlet. I learned that if I was able to find a five-minute break, where I could let everything go and concentrate on nothing—or on something that had nothing to do with what I was in the midst of—, that's all I needed to be able to continue on. The breaks didn't have to be all that many—but just a few here and there—and they would work their magic. Give it a whirl when everything around you is turning to you know what. It works wonders.

Let's move on to Bank of America.

Now that we've set the stage for the process that one must go through to finally get to a point where the creditor will negotiate a settlement of a defaulted account, this story will be a lot shorter.

Bank of America was always a good outfit to deal with—from the initial conversation of why all of a sudden I ceased making payments on the two BofA credit cards I had with them, through my explanation of what had gone down, etc.—they were always "good" to deal with.

I will say this about the credit-card companies: You will find that some will tell you they have some sort of financial-assistance plan that can be put in place for people who have some incident come up that prevents them from making their payments, but from my experience, as you will see further on, it's all a load of crap.

Back to BofA. Once I had gotten sufficiently delinquent on my account to where they were going to "turn it over" (Latin for "*sell*"?) to a collection agency (which, in this instance, amounted to about six months past due), things started happening. What was encouraging and uplifting to me with BofA was that, when I got to that point, toward the end of April, I received a phone call from one of the last-ditch negotiators, and the conversation was very, very different.

He started it all with this comment: "Mr. Bowler, in looking over your payment history on these two credit cards, your payment record was always perfect. Never a problem. Then, all of a sudden, your payments just stopped! Could you tell me what happened to cause this?"

Well, I told him the whole story, and he actually listened to what I was telling him. At the end of my comments, he said, "That's awful." Then he proceeded to say that, with as good a customer as I had been with them over the years, Bank of America owed me something. Wow. He actually said that. And he said that he understood exactly what had happened to cause us not to be able to make our payments, and to show good faith on his/their part, he offered to settle our two credit card debts at forty cents on the dollar. Now I was encouraged. I told him that while I appreciated his kindness, I still could not come up with that much money to pay that settlement amount. I told him that I felt like I could assemble some funds over a ninety-day period as we continued to liquidate personal assets and that I could commit to paying a total of $12,000 (which was about 30 percent of what we owed) through three payments of $4,000 each per month. Thankfully he said, "OK"! I asked him to set that out in writing (*always* do that, so there's no question after the agreement has been made and you are in process of taking care of your end of the bargain). He did so, and, once we both signed, we had a deal.

Over that period of time, I was able to assemble the funds from selling assets and liquidating the majority of what I had left in my 401(k) retirement account, and, within the agreed-upon ninety days, I paid them the amount we had agreed to and received a letter confirming the full settlement of the two credit-card debts.

Thank you, Bank of America. I will always appreciate how you helped me out on these two debts.

Now, let's talk about Wells Fargo.

Shades of Capital One. Here was another instance of getting a working-capital line of credit over the phone. As you will see, however, there is one significant difference, and it turned out to be a very important one.

I had received one of those "you are pre-qualified" letters we all have received, that advised me that we had access to a Wells Fargo business line of credit up to $100,000 that looked pretty good. So I called to get further information, and decided that it was pretty good, and went ahead with a telephone application, and—wouldn't you know it—I got approved for a $90,000 loan. They sent me everything I needed to be able to draw down the funds, and I did so.

Since there was never a formal loan application that we filled out and signed, and since there was never a promissory note that we signed, etc., my attorney gave me the same advice on this debt as he did on the Capital One debt: Don't pay it! It's a business debt, and, with the business closure, there was no way they could come against us personally. They, too, were out of luck.

I took the same approach with Wells Fargo that I had with Capital One. But, unfortunately, they had one piece of "documentation" against us that I had forgotten about. They had the presence of mind, when they told me on the phone that we had been approved, to get Julie on the line with me and explain to us that this debt required us to be personally liable for the debt. They asked us if we both understood that and agreed to it. In that phone conversation, we did understand that requirement, and we did agree to our personal liability. Then the funds came as promised.

I had not remembered that important piece, and, so, when I asked the collection person to prove that we were personally liable, I was sent a CD containing our phone conversation, which clearly recorded everything just as I described.

I took that CD to my attorney, and after we listened to the recorded conversation, he told me that, while we might still be able to avoid personal liability, it would take some legal action to do so and that the statutes in Colorado were such that this phone-call acceptance of personal liability would very possibly prevail. While I was of a mind to just go for a court proceeding, in the end, I let my better judgment prevail.

Thus it was that I went back to the negotiating table with Wells Fargo. We started throwing numbers around, but they made it clear that, no matter what, they could not and would not discount my debt by more than $50,000. I was in the process of selling our second home, which was the sole remaining source of funds that I could use to pay them off, so I successfully did a slow negotiation that took us through the closing of the sale of that piece of real estate, and it gave us the funds needed to settle this debt.

It is important to know that, with all of the settlements that I negotiated and completed, one of the terms of the agreements was that the debtor would notify the credit bureaus of the settlement of their debt and make sure I got the benefit of as good a rating as possible for standing up to the plate and paying them off with enough money to affect a settlement and not have them incur a total write-off. That action paid off well, as, through it all, my credit rating at the end of the process was not damaged as badly as I initially thought it was going to be.

Another point to remember: Keep copious notes, and as much documentation as you can gather. Not always were the debt settlements shown correctly on my credit report, and having the documentation that was assembled in the negotiation and settlement of the debts was extremely valuable in getting the records straight and thus come out with a fairly decent credit rating.

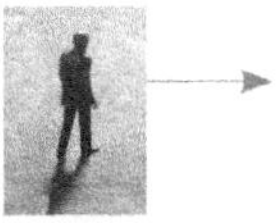

Chapter 14

SELLING THE PERSONAL ASSETS

As I said earlier, Julie and I had to sell and/or liquidate as many assets as we could to get these debts taken care of. We knew this was going to be part of the self-managed liquidation process, and, after all, we needed to be willing to take it in the chops if we were asking creditors to do the same.

On December 31, 2010, we closed the sale of one of those assets. Julie's mother's home in Berthoud, Colorado, which we had purchased from Julie's other siblings after her mother passed away. Julie loved that house. It had been built in 1906 and was literally the Gateway to Berthoud, on the main drag connecting Berthoud with Interstate 25. She had allowed the community to use that house for special community events and tried to do as much with it as she could in our stressed-out condition. In the end, we could not keep up on the payments on the loan we took out to provide funds to the company, and we had to let it go. During our ownership of the property, the City of Berthoud had decided to take part of the property for the construction of a roundabout. While that adversely impacted the value and ultimate sales price we were able to garner for the home, over a one-year period of negotiation with the city, we were able to come out with a decent settlement. After we closed on the sale, we were able pay off the delinquent loan with Chase. Chase was brutal throughout the delinquent payment period, both with the mortgage loan on the Berthoud property and with what I would consider to be close to harassment in collection efforts on our two Chase credit cards.

Having the funds in hand and the Chase mortgage paid in full, we immediately went down to the Chase Bank near our home, and, with a somewhat slightly spectacular display of emotion on my part, proceeded to pay off those two credit-card debts and advise the audience (which included employees and customers) that we would not do business with Chase again if it were the last bank on the face of the earth.

That left us with only one piece of accumulated real estate left that we could sell and still save our home: Our "cabin" outside of Sedalia, Colorado.

We had purchased that beautiful house on five acres of wooded land bordering the Pike National Forest just southwest of Sedalia some ten years earlier. We used it as a second home and enjoyed the quiet peacefulness of the home and surroundings. We became friends with one or two of the homeowners in the area, and it was a totally different way of life up there.

There are some stories about this property that are interesting, but I'll keep it short.

In January of 2009, I had a feeling that I needed to go visit the cabin. We hadn't been there for a while, and it had been very cold, and I just felt the need to check and see how things were.

I got a bad feeling in the pit of my stomach when I had trouble opening the door to the lower level of the home, which was used as the main entrance to the house. I quickly found out why when I finally was able to get the door opened and walked right into two inches of water that had pooled in the entire lower level. Ceiling tiles and the insulation that was above the tiles were all hanging down in the furnace room (which was the first room you went through to get to the rest of the house) and throughout the rest of the finished lower level. What a mess!!!

A water pipe had burst in the kitchen on the second (main) level, just above the furnace room, and our well had been pumping water constantly for an unknown amount of time, doing an amazing amount of damage. I walked through the water in the lower level up to the main level to see what had happened. That's where I discovered the broken water line under the kitchen sink that was pouring water through the break. We had no way of knowing how long this had been going on, but I felt it was probably at least a couple of weeks and maybe as much as a month.

I then found a flashlight in a kitchen drawer, and took it with me so I could see into the somewhat-hidden place in the lower level to find the switch to the pump so that I could turn it off. When I got back downstairs, I found that the batteries to the flashlight were dead (of course!). By this time, I was pretty thoroughly disgusted and depressed. I looked at the light switch by the washer and dryer, which would turn on a light so that I could see where the pump switch was located. After considering that I was standing in several inches of water and that water was coming down all over me through the ceiling, and knowing what could happen if this didn't go well, I decided, "What the hell!", and reached over and turned on the light switch so I could see the pump.

Well, nothing bad happened with that move, so now having light to be able to see by, I turned off the pump, and the water coming down through the ceiling slowly came to a stop. That began a six-month demolition and renovation project that ended with us totally remodeling the cabin. This turned out to be a blessing. Unknown to us at the time, in the not-too-distant future, we were going to have to sell our dream home.

Being a licensed real estate broker in the State of Colorado, I decided I would list our property for sale through my real estate brokerage company, Alegro Investments. On April 30, 2011, I put the listing into the Denver MultiList service, planted the signs, and we were now on the market.

It took a while in the market we were stuck in, but after consecutive reductions in the asking price, in July, we finally got a contract negotiated and were heading toward a closing which would provide the funding to pay off that last loan with Wells Fargo.

While we were under contract and the buyer was doing due diligence, I got a call from the buyer's agent telling me that we had a problem at the house. There had been some heavy rainstorms up in that area, and, one night, one of the trees that was close to the house came toppling down, and on its way down, it just happened to fall on the main electrical supply line that ran to the home and tore all the electrical equipment off the side of the house.

Are you kidding me???!!!

Twice with two properties!!??

So I went down there ASAP, and, yes, there it was. The good news was that I now had experience in dealing with this particular kind of problem, complete with a well-qualified electrical contractor that I had used to remedy the same exact situation with our plant up in Denver. So, without hesitation, I called him up and had him come down, and after expressing his disbelief that this could happen twice to one person, he said he could take care of it with no problem.

Well, we got that all fixed, put a new roof on the home, and ended up closing on the sale of that property.

We now had sold all of our assets we could get our hands on to do any good, and we had the funds in the bank to take care of settling the last debt on the list.

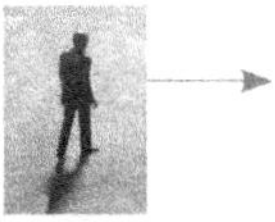

Chapter 15

THE CONCLUSION

Today is Friday, September 30, 2011. It was exactly two years ago today that I locked the doors on our business and stepped into the darkness.

This morning, I paid the agreed-upon settlement amount to pay off the Wells Fargo business loan made to Phoenix Custom Apparel. The amount tendered: $37,338.63, on a debt that they had on their records at an $87,338.63 balance. That took care of paying off the final big debt left from the company closure.

So, as of this afternoon, we have been able to go from a total debt obligation of $1,835,895, with monthly payment obligations of $27,985, to a grand-total debt of $251,983, with total monthly payments of $2,368.

We still have some work to do, but this is manageable.

I had previously scheduled a lunch with Paul Kluck for today, September 30, 2011, at La Fogata, and I didn't realize until we were almost through the lunch what the significance of today was. It was the two-year anniversary of the company closure. It was most appropriate having the lunch with Paul, as he'd been my sidekick in this whole odyssey, constantly being there through the whole ordeal.

My purpose of our lunch was to share with him all the gory details that occurred during the seventy-five days it took to get the cabin sale closed. But, after going through all that, I suddenly realized that today was the two-year anniversary of closing down the company and that "it was all over."

I had a meltdown at that moment as I shared with Paul what the day, and the morning's event, signified. And part of the significance was: My "full-time job" for the past two years was done. Over. Gone.

Interestingly, Paul then shared that he never doubted that I would pull this off. He said that rather than just throw in the towel and "quit," my resolve to get the job done and my statement to him at the beginning of the journey that this was going to be "my full-time job" convinced him right then and there that I would be victorious, and that my self-managed liquidation would have a successful closure experience. He said for me to always remember that closing the company down and going through all that I did was not a defeat but most assuredly a success, and that I should be proud of that success.

What a friend, and business partner.

Thank you, Paul, for sticking with me through thick and thin, for giving me the support you did, and for the sense that I could feel for these past two years that you did have confidence in my ability to bring this off, and to actually "pull the light in after me."

And so can you, whoever is reading this book.

The End (?)

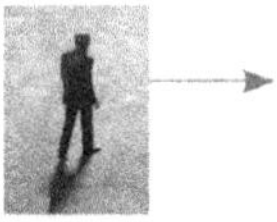

Chapter 16

REFLECTIONS

Ooops.

Not quite. There's more to share.

First, some thoughts from inside [me]:

Some of the things that helped me through it all, and kept me going:

Music became really important.

The song "I Have a Dream" kept me going while at Phoenix. Thank you, ABBA, and for you, Matt, who'd introduced me to that song years earlier.

I started up a sort of "follow-up" business to take care of some of the Phoenix customers who came to me after the closing and still wanted to do business with me, purchasing product that I had created using an offshore manufacturer. I had leased an office near our home to conduct that business out of, and in December of 2010, when things were pretty tough, I remember tearfully hanging upon every note and word of the song of Merle Haggard called "If We Make It Through December." That song really held me up through all that was hanging over my head.

All through the two years of darkness, "Smile," by Nat "King" Cole, was a constant companion.

My wife and I went and saw the movie *The Wrestler*. The title song, "The Wrestler," so powerfully performed by Bruce Springsteen, became "my song"—the song that I felt most accurately described Bruce Bowler. I am listening to that song now as I write these words, and it still so touches what I feel deep inside of me.

When we closed Phoenix down, Matt sent out an e-mail to me and Mary (and maybe others) attaching what he suggested would be an appropriate and meaningful and whole wraparound song entitled "EXOGENESIS: Symphony Part 3 (Redemption)." What beautiful music—sweet, soulful, touching, and then it gets into a crescendo with the words "*Let's start over again …. Why can't we start it over again?*" What an impact it had then, and even more so today, as I look back and realize that that is exactly what we all did, every wonderful employee of Phoenix Custom Apparel. We all started over again. Thank you, Matt, for your loving in-tune-ness.

If you are having difficulties, try grabbing on to songs that give you encouragement and strength and an emotional shoulder to rest your weary head on. Music can do wonders to keep you going.

I also want to tell you how I feel that this whole thing coming to pass was nothing short of a miracle. When Paul e-mailed me the last contract offer on the purchase of the plant, he included this comment: "God is watching over you." Yes, Paul, I do believe you were right. So, I clearly want to give God, the

Creator, the Universal Mind and Spirit, the well-deserved credit for bringing this all together—for the blessings, strength, help from others, wisdom, insight, courage, and "increase" that were given to me and my efforts to get this done.

A last reflective note:

The gentleman who put my lease together to get my new business into its offices quickly became a good friend. After I had been a tenant for some time, I began to negotiate for some back-room space to help our shipments coming in and out of the office be more efficient. The negotiations became harder and harder—confrontive, even angry at times, between us. After one of the more combative sessions conducted in my office one day, as he sat across my desk from me, he became quiet and, with a surprise on his face at how aggressive I was, just stopped and looked at me. As I observed him, all of a sudden, I came face to face with the reality that I was still operating in the "fighting mode" that I had been in for two years. I had become a person I did not want to be. I realized that I needed to let go of my fighting mode and come back to who I was, and wanted to be.

I then invited him to stay for a bit and poured drinks for us; and we sat and talked about what I had just come to realize. After he left, I put together the PowerPoint piece that I then printed out and hung on my wall by my computer, so I could see it all the time. It has helped me make the needed course corrections in my life, attitude, and character to bring me back to me.

Here's the printout……

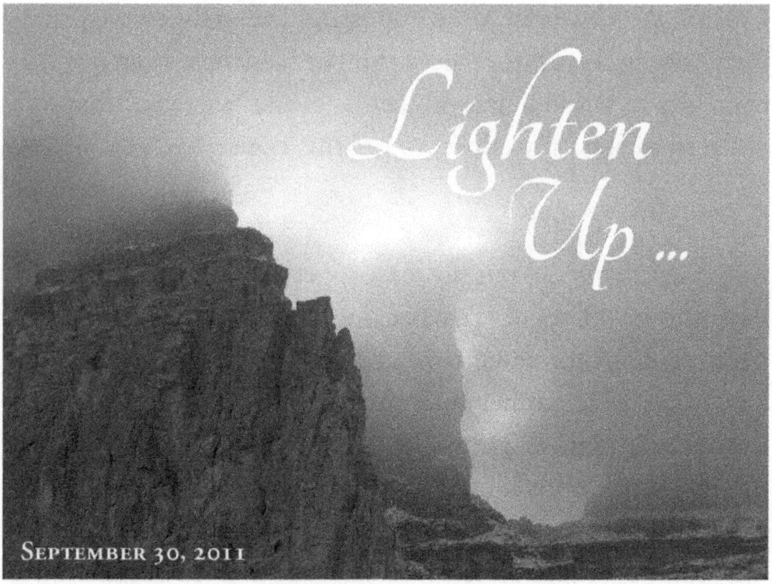
Lighten Up ...
September 30, 2011

Chapter 17

THE US BANK MARATHON

Well, it wasn't quite over yet.

Friday, June 29, 2012.

On June 29, 2011, we closed on the sale of our plant at 3660 East 40th Avenue. What an ending that was. And, as I said earlier, that closing took place just days prior to the Foreclosure Sale was to take place.

Then there was the ending after paying off "all" the remaining debts on September 30, 2011.

It is now June 29, 2012, exactly one year to the date of the closing of the sale of our building and paying off the debts against it, and I am back in the saddle, paying off—literally and *finally*—the last two remaining debts of the business (not counting the loan against our home, which was taken out to fund Phoenix as a "business debt").

You see, there were these two "leftover" debts that had sort of been taken care of that reared their ugly heads. Here's that story:

During the time Phoenix was functioning, there were two US Bank credit cards that were used from time to time to acquire fabric, take care of bills, etc., essentially providing additional lines of credit to generate needed funding.

One of those credit cards was created under Phoenix Motorsports and was used to do what credit cards do for a business, this one being the operation of our semi-professional drag-racing activities. That balance had been paid in full when we shut down our racing operation, but since it had a nice limit on it, as the need arose to provide funding for Phoenix Custom Apparel, it was used accordingly.

The other credit card was one that was created for the apparel business.

Sometime prior to 2011, I had ceased making payments on these credit cards, just like all the other company debts, since there were no funds to make those payments and also, since, unless the debts were in a delinquent status, you couldn't negotiate any settlement arrangement with the creditors. So we endured the ceaseless phone calls, etc., and just bided our time, waiting until there was a point where we could negotiate some sort of reasonable settlement or restructure to resolve the debts.

On December 29, 2010, I succeeded in establishing an interest rate/payment structure under US Bank's "Hardship Program" that dropped our interest rate on both credit cards to 7.4 percent and lowered our total payments on these two debts from a total of $704 per month down to $423. That action took us out of a delinquent status, stopped late fees from accruing, stopped the incessant collection phone calls, and started reducing the unpaid principal balances pretty nicely.

On September 28, 2011, since we had a few bucks left over from selling everything, I called US Bank to see if we could do some sort of settlement, whereby I could just pay the debts off and get rid of them. But, true to form, I was told "Current accounts are not eligible for a settlement," even though they were in the hardship program.

So, we made our mind up to keep on paying the hardship-program payments as had been restructured, let them pay out over time, and be done with them. Therefore, we felt they were "taken care of."

Wrongamungo.

You can imagine my surprise when we received the following "Good News!" letter from US Bank (there was one for each credit card, but I'm showing only one as they both read exactly the same):

Cardmember Service PO Box 108, St Louis, MO 63166-9801

usbank

January 05, 2012

PHOENIX CUSTOM APPRL
BRUCE BOWLER
3905 S WABASH ST
DENVER, CO 80237-1718

Account No: 4336940003141649
Balance: $15,744.64

Dear PHOENIX CUSTOM APPRL :

Good News! We are pleased to announce that your participation in our Special Payment Relief Program has been successfully completed. We greatly appreciate your dedication in this program for the entire term.

Now that the special fixed rate APR is ending, the original terms of your credit card account will take effect. Your new interest rate will be Prime + 11.74% for purchases and Prime + 20.74% for cash advances. Your new minimum monthly payment will be adjusted accordingly.

If you have any questions or concerns regarding the new terms of your credit card account, please call us at 1-877-838-4347. Thanks again for your commitment to this Special Payment Relief Program. All of us are looking forward to serving you.

Sincerely,

Cardmember Services

This is an attempt to collect a debt. Any information obtained will be used for that purpose.

Are you kidding me!!??#@

We had sucked it up and faithfully made the payments on these two debts for a year, and, as a reward, we were now being taken off the program, the interest rate kicked back up, and the payments raised back up? Wow.

Thanks for being so grateful!

And, just where was the ability to make these increased payments magically supposed to come from? What is there in their wisdom that I am missing, such that we now are just miraculously going to be capable of paying this greatly increased amount?

When I called the bank, I was told that these letters were not supposed to have gone out—that I should have been contacted by someone in the collection department to discuss going off the hardship program, but the system failed. Would I like to talk to someone about going back on the hardship program?

No. Time to play *the game* again.

Time to let the damn things go back into a delinquent status so that I can once again see if we can find some level of settlement and get rid of these debts and our connection to US Bank. So, we stopped making payments, and the collection phone calls resumed.

About March, it seemed time to start up the process of either a settlement or another hardship program, but with a long-term twist. I will say categorically that US Bank has been the most hardheaded, stubborn, difficult creditor we had the misfortune to deal with in the entire group of creditors.

Anyway, the attempt to come to an agreed-upon settlement percentage failed, even with a 60 percent offer (which was the highest-percent settlement offer I had made to any of our unsecured creditors, all of whom had agreed to lower settlements). So, I made a payment-restructuring offer of 0 percent, sixty months, payments paid monthly at whatever the balances were at that time, divided by sixty. That way, they got 100 percent of their money back—it just took a while. And, we could live with that budget.

They came back with a new hardship program deal that said 4.9 percent interest, sixty months, monthly payments to be drafted out of our bank account until paid in full, with a total payment of $611 per month. That amount was a bit of a choker, but I was getting tired of this game by now, and in a moment of weakness, on April 19, 2012, I said, "OK," and that payment structure began.

The Final Piece of the Financial Puzzle

We're now up to June 29, 2012. It is 9:48 a.m., and I am waiting for the phone call from Stewart Title to tell me to come pick up the checks that I will then take over to US Bank to pay these two credit cards *in full*—one hundred cents on the dollar—and be rid of them and the last of the business debts.

How did that come about?

Well, after putting the finishing touches on the US Bank hardship program, and getting those monthly payments up and running with the credit cards back into a current status, I started making my financial calculations to see what we could do to restructure our remaining debt load and perhaps further lighten the burden of our monthly outgo.

The first mortgage on our home was at an interest rate of 5.75 percent, and the market was well below that rate. Perhaps it was time to consider refinancing that debt and, if at all possible, include in that refinance the liquidation of the two US Bank business credit-card debts.

You're kidding—right, Bruce? After all the things that you have been through to pay off all the debts you had from the closing of the business? What are you thinking? Your credit rating has to be trashed!

But, it was worth the investigation to see if such a concept was possible.

So, I called the one person I knew I could trust and rely on to run a current credit report on Julie and me, analyze it, sit down with me to go over it in detail, and then advise me on whether or not pursuing a refinance of our home loan would be reasonable.

Who was that person? Gayle Campbell, Vice President of Underwriting of Universal Lending Corporation. I had actually hired Gayle as a loan underwriter when I was still half-owner and CEO of Universal Lending. She took over the management of that department, we had a great relationship while I was at ULC, and we never let that relationship go. She was a great underwriter and a fantastic lady, so why not call her and see what she thought?

I made that call and went to lunch with her at La Fogata to go over the credit report and see what she thought.

I was pleasantly surprised. Our credit ratings were still pretty good. Mine was a 648, and Julie's was a 718. The credit report showed pretty good, and what it taught me was that, if you just plow ahead, work with the creditors, and get them taken care of as best as you can, then somehow it works out.

Gayle said that if all the planets came into alignment (meaning that the appraisal on our home came in OK and our income was good in relationship to our total debts), we had a decent shot at pulling it off.

We made our loan application, got the appraisal ordered, gathered all the financial information together, presented that to underwriting, and lo and behold, on Monday, June 25, 2012 we closed on our new loan with Universal Lending Corporation. With the three-day Right of Rescission holding up the disbursement of funds, we had to wait until today, Friday, June 29, to have the title company make the disbursements on the loan. This will include paying off our existing mortgage and writing the two checks to US Bank that I will personally take over to them to pay off the last two business debts. The good news with all that is, in addition to finally liquidating all the business debts, our monthly payment obligations will drop by $800 per month, which is a significant amount.

That's the plan. Let's see how this all plays out today....

1:35 p.m. The checks are ready for pickup!! Yes!

I picked up the checks, made copies for my file, went to US Bank, walked right up to the teller, and paid these two debts off, in full!

An aside: I was prompted to call Paul Kluck, whose office is just across the street from US Bank, and asked if he could join me for a drink up the street. He said "Sure," so I picked him up. Interestingly, today was the anniversary of the closing of our sale of the plant, and in addition to recounting that significant event, I shared that today had another event that gave reason for celebration and told him this latest story.

It was great and as we left the bar, in the parking lot, he smiled at me and said, "You're on your way back!"

Yes, indeed.

Chapter 18

THE SUBLIMATION EQUIPMENT LEASE CRISIS

I almost put a "The End" at the end of the previous chapter. It's a good thing I didn't.

This reminds me of those horror movies where every time you kill the monster, somehow the damn thing comes back to life and heads right at you.

Back when we stepped into the darkness and pulled the plug, the first ray of light (at least it seemed so at the time) was that I immediately had a buyer for our most expensive equipment and biggest business debt: the sublimation equipment we had purchased less than a year before the day we closed the business.

You may recall that we had been doing subcontracting sublimation for a company here in Denver. They were very pleased with our product, and their sales were doing well in their niche. We had become friends with the two owners, Craig Pena and Jay Salas, who owned several businesses. As previously mentioned, Jay happened to come over to pick up an order the afternoon we were having our "good-bye luncheon" with our employees, and when he asked what we were going to do with our sublimation equipment and I told him we were going to sell it, he immediately said, "We'll buy it!"

I thought, *Wahoo! This might work out after all.* So, I proceeded to work with Craig, who was the business person in the partnership, to draft a complex agreement for them to take over not only our sublimation equipment but our entire sublimation division, including our existing book of business. The "heart" of the sublimation process is the digital graphic-art capabilities, and included in the agreement was the setting up of our VP of Art & Design, Matt, as their subcontractor to seamlessly give them that key piece. This agreement set them up to be able to find past customers' artwork, do new design work, and create the vital print templates that would be used to actually sublimate (print) the image onto the fabric.

As part of that agreement, Craig and Jay and their newly formed apparel business, called "J-C Apparel," took over our lease. We applied for and received the approval of AEL Financial, LLC, who owned the lease with the one-dollar buyout contract we structured when we acquired the equipment. With that approval, Craig and Jay assumed and agreed to pay the balance of that contract.

I agreed to let J-C rent space in our building to operate their equipment and generate income while they were setting up a new production facility in another location. By doing so, Mary and Matt could give them training on operating the printer and heat press, while we got a little income for providing them production facilities. This worked out well for all parties, and within two or three months, they moved all the sublimation equipment into their new facilities and emptied out our space.

This was a big load off our shoulders, and helped set the protocol for our selling off the other two major "pieces" of our business: The firesuit division and the embroidery division.

This sale of the sublimation equipment took place in October of 2009.

Things seemed to go well with that transaction, until sometime after the assumption of the lease contract took place, Julie and I started getting late-payment notices from AEL Financial from time to time, stating that J-C Apparel had failed to make one or more payments on the contract, that they were notifying us since we were still Guarantors on the Contract, and thus had personal liability on that debt (which, at the time of our sale to them, was about $80,000).

As a point of clarification, when we were negotiating the assumption of the lease, I asked for Julie and me to be released from that guarantee but was told we were *not* going to be released from that guarantee. I had to think about that, but, in the end, we decided that we really had no choice but to go forward with the sale, get that obligation transferred to J-C Apparel, and hope like hell they did well in their business and would end up paying it off over the next four years as per our agreement.

When we would get those notification letters, which continued to come over time, I would get hold of Jay or Craig or both, and we'd have some communication about "what are you guys doing, and when are you going to take care of paying these lease payments," etc., and they would pony up the money to make the payments—but, unfortunately, not in a totally consistent manner. There were often broken promises, lack of communication from the guys, and fights between them and AEL. I would step in and talk with the collections people at AEL and work with them in every way I could to get the payments from J-C, and keep things afloat. As things got worse and worse, I even tried to get AEL to let me become a part of their "team" to resolve this situation, take possession of the equipment, and resell it. That boat did not float. I even considered taking it back and restarting the Phoenix book of business and going from there. But, after all considerations, I just kept doing what I had been doing and hoped it would all work out.

Then, at 10:15 a.m. on December 24, 2012 (yes, Virginia, that was Christmas Eve Day), Julie and I each got FedEx Standard Overnight deliveries to our home containing a letter giving us "formal notification of default under your lease agreement and applicable guaranty with AEL Financial, LLC. Your lease is now past due for $20,564.09. As a result, the entire accelerated balance of **$49,253.73, plus any outstanding taxes and fees, is now due and payable immediately. You have ten (10) days from the date of this letter to resolve your default with AEL Financial, LLC.**" The emphasized bold lettering was actually in this letter.

You can see the letter on the next page.

Well, a very Merry Christmas to you, too, AEL Financial!

First, I sent off a pretty scathing e-mail to Craig and Jay, requesting that we meet right away to discuss this situation and figure out what we were all going to do about it.

AEL Financial, LLC
Box 88046
Milwaukee, WI 53288-0046

December 21, 2012

Bruce Bowler
3905 S Wabash St
Denver, CO 80237

RE: Lease No. 28059616

This letter is your formal notification of default under your lease agreement and applicable guaranty with AEL Financial, LLC. Your lease is now past due for $20,564.09. As a result, the entire accelerated balance of **$49,253.73, plus any outstanding taxes and fees, is now due and payable immediately.**

You have ten (10) days from the date of this letter to resolve your default with AEL Financial, LLC. If left unresolved, your defaulted contract will be referred for immediate further actions up to and including transfer to legal counsel, notification to applicable credit reporting agency services, and return of the equipment to AEL Financial, LLC. If AEL is forced to take these actions, you will also be responsible for additional costs including legal fees and expenses, court costs, collection fees, and equipment return fees.

To avoid these imminent actions, you must resolve your default within ten (10) days of the date of this notice. Failure to comply will leave us no alternative but to take immediate and appropriate steps to protect our interests.

Yours truly,
AEL Financial, LLC

Michelle Casey
Risk Management
866-761-2433

Then, I placed a call to Michelle Casey, Risk Management, AEL Financial, LLC, who had been so kind as to write and deliver these unique Christmas Greetings. I was unable to reach her. Of course. It was Christmas Eve. I left a voice message and called it a day.

As you can imagine, that Christmas was emotionally dropped down a notch or two. But, you know, we had been through this for two years since the closing and gone through a lot of debt negotiations, so we were pretty toughened and knew the drill.

The huge difference this time, however, was that we didn't have any reserves or cash or other assets to dispose of to try to come up with this kind of money.

For the first time in this whole experience, I found myself with the realization that we really may have to declare bankruptcy and face whatever consequences that would bring, and I thought: *Are you serious?!?! We have gone through all that we have gone through and made it this far without declaring bankruptcy, and now this comes at us, which may be the one last piece that could bring us to that sorry conclusion.* Wow. What a feeling that was.

But you had great training from what we had gone through, so suck it up, Bruce, and deal with this like you did the others.

As it was, on December 28, 2012, I put together a three-page letter that I sent to addresses in Milwaukee, Wisconsin, and Portland, Oregon. I sent it to both of those places just to make sure it got to Ms. Casey or someone else in authority in the AEL organization.

Thus began the process.

Here's that letter:

BRUCE BOWLER

3905 South Wabash Street
Denver, Colorado 80237

(303) 770-2171 (Home) (303) 758-0707 (Work)
(303) 886-5211 (Cell) (303) 758-3371 (FAX)

December 28, 2012
Ms. Michelle Casey
Risk Management
AEL Financial, LLC
Box 88046
Milwaukee, WI 53288-0046

RE: Lease No. 28059616

Dear Ms. Casey:

At 10:15 am on the morning of the 24th of December, my wife and I received your Demand Letter dated December 21, 2012 that you had sent to us via FedEx Overnight Delivery to our home.

At 10:40 am on the 24th of December, I placed a call to you to obtain your e-mail address and/or your FAX number to be able to set up a more fluid communication network with you. I have not received a phone call back from you, so I am writing this letter.

I want to make it a matter of record that I have responded to the phone calls from your company from Shannon, as well as Beverly Harris, to do all I could to assist them in their collection efforts being made upon Craig Pena and Jay Salas, owners of J-C Apparel, who assumed and agreed to pay the AEL Lease referenced above when they purchased the equipment and customer base from Phoenix Custom Apparel back in 2009.

In my last conversation with your company, which was with Shannon on November 28, 2012, I advised her that my wife and I were not in the financial position to be able to bring the lease payments current or pay of the debt. We are both in our 70s and just recently wound up settling the final debts associated with the closing of Phoenix Custom Apparel back in September of 2009, and going through that process has pretty much wiped out all of our assets. We have and are continuing to restructure our own debts to be able to make ends meet, and there is no way we can take on the AEL lease obligation financially.

However, I did tell Shannon that the best way that I could be of help to AEL would be to be brought in as a member of your "team" to assist in the acquisition of the equipment and in selling it, with the goal of paying you off in full. Here are the reasons that I feel I can be of benefit to you in this regard:

1. I am intimately familiar with every piece of equipment that is encumbered by the AEL Lease. I personally know what it can do and the quality of every piece.
2. I still have a lot of contacts in the sublimation industry and am very willing to go into the market to find buyers for that equipment.
3. I live in Denver and can assist in the physical acquisition of the equipment. I can be instrumental in finding a place for that equipment to be stored and taken care of while the marketing process is taking place.
4. Because of all of the above, I believe that the costs associated with acquiring the equipment and the price that can be obtained from selling said equipment can all be accomplished with the very best financial results possible.

When I related all of the above to Shannon, she said that she would "funnel it up the line." This is to memorialize not only my *offer* to be of assistance but also my request to be involved in the acquisition and liquidation of the equipment, if it comes to that.

I also expressed my wonder at why AEL had not pursued this course of action.

Regardless, I am aware of what Craig and Jay are trying to do to take care of their obligation. And, I am sympathetic to what you and they are doing to give them the opportunity to bring this debt current. I requested that Craig and Jay meet with me after receiving your December 24th Demand Letter, which they did. They told me that they had made one partial payment to you and were making another one, I believe today, and that they have been and will continue to be in contact with Shannon to take care of you. I was told they were also trying to refinance the obligation in order to pay you in full, reduce the monthly payment by at least half, and that they were in the process of working that refinancing out.

During our meeting, I told them that, having been in the real estate lending industry for some 40 years, I watched with interest at the attempts by the government and the lending community to help people with mortgage debt with whom they were having difficulty handling work-out solutions by refinancing that debt and reducing the monthly payments.

I suggested that Craig ask Shannon if there was a possibility that AEL Financial could re-cast their lease, with the new amount being the total amount due AEL of $49,253.73 for a 5-year term and even offer to do this restructuring at the existing rate of interest. I said that, if they could do that with you, their payment obligation could drop probably in half, and they could much more afford to make the payments. And, coupling all of this with the benefit of being able to bring a delinquent account current through this re-casting of the lease, I couldn't imagine a better win-win solution to the current situation. They agreed that this would be a great program for them, and would certainly do it if they could.

Craig said he was scheduled to contact Shannon Friday (today) and that part of his conversation with her would be to ask if the lease could be re-cast as we discussed.

Craig just called me a few minutes ago and told me that he did in fact talk to Shannon and that, when he brought up this concept of a lease re-structuring, he was told that it would not be possible, that AEL did not do re-casting of any of their leases, and that this would not be a possible solution to the situation.

Craig and Jay will continue to do what they can to bring you current and/or pay you off. And I commend them for that.

However, with what has been done in the rest of the financial markets to help out situations exactly like what Craig and Jay are experiencing, I really don't understand why a company like yours would not be willing to consider re-casting their lease at a debt that is virtually half of what it was when it was first structured and still has the entire equipment package as collateral.

With this letter, I am asking for three things:

1. Your e-mail address and FAX number.
2. That AEL reconsider the possibility of re-casting the existing lease as outlined above.
3. If, at some point in time, AEL decides to pursue the acquisition and liquidation of the lease collateral, that I be brought in to assist in that process.

Thank you for your consideration. I will await your reply.
Bruce Bowler

• • •

I won't take you through the long, tedious, exasperating experience of dealing with AEL Financial on this matter. I'll just give you the highlights.

First, I never received a phone call or a response from Ms. Casey. Surprise.

Then, on January 16, 2013, I received a phone call from a man by the name of Jake Randolph. He said he was AEL's Litigation Auditor, and advised me that if, within the next seventy-two hours something definitive with evidence of the capability of performing whatever they were told did not take place, he was going to send the file to an attorney in Denver to file the papers in Court to bring a lawsuit against Julie and me and Craig and Jay for collection of the account, plus attorney's fees (estimated to be from $12,000 to $15,000). He asked if I could bring the account current, and I said "No." He said the only thing left for us to do was for us to file a Chapter 7 Bankruptcy.

I asked Mr. Randolph why in the world AEL had not proceeded to take possession of the equipment before allowing it to go ten months delinquent? He admitted they "made a mistake" in not going forward with taking legal action when the account went to the four-month delinquent status long ago and that they should have done something earlier. He informed me that AEL would never have agreed to the assumption of the lease without having our personal guarantees in place. It was pretty obvious that he had seen our credit report showing what we had done to take care of the Phoenix obligations in its past and that, because of that, Julie and I had become AEL's primary target in solving their delinquent-lease problem.

I asked him to hold off until I could have a meeting with Craig and Jay, and then I would get back to him. He agreed to do so. I was also advised by Mr. Randolph that, "I will no longer deal with Craig Pena and Jay Salas. I am through listening to and counting on their broken promises, and I will have communication and negotiations with only you on this matter." I understood, and when I told Craig and Jay what Mr. Randolph said, they also understood and knew they had burned that bridge because of their past conduct.

I met with Craig and Jay, and pointed out to them what all of us stood to lose if this went to repossession/court action/etc., and that, with the total amount of payments we had jointly made on this contract over its life and were now less than a year away from paying it off, it made absolutely no sense whatsoever to let this happen.

Everyone agreed, and through the process of dual negotiation with AEL on one side and J-C Apparel on the other side, the following was structured and agreed to between Bowler Enterprises and J-C Apparel:

- Bruce Bowler and Bowler Enterprises would now deal directly with AEL Financial until this thing was over.
- Craig and Jay would raise $23,000 to bring the payments to a current status.
- All funds would be given to Bowler Enterprises, which would then remit said funds under the Bowler Enterprises company bank account to AEL Financial.
- From here on out, all payments would be made to Bowler Enterprises in a timely manner, so that the money necessary to bring the payments current and to make all future monthly payments could be remitted to AEL.

- Upon payment of the final contract installment for the December 1, 2013 payment, accompanied by the payment of one dollar to effect the buyout provision in the lease contract to obtain title to the equipment, once Bruce and Julie Bowler obtained Title to the equipment, that Title would be transferred to J-C Apparel and they would then own it free and clear.

With the J-C agreement in place, I structured an Agreement between AEL Financial and Bowler Enterprises. AEL had been so lax in every respect on this transaction, including giving me no less than three different amounts of the "real" amount that was due them on the Contract, that I put forth a very detailed, point-by-point Agreement of what Julie and I would agree to. I sent it off to Mr. Randolph and requested that he have my Agreement reproduced on AEL stationery, and then sign it as their authorized representative. Upon receiving said signed Agreement, Julie and I would then counter-sign it, upon which we could, and would, go forward to get this matter resolved. Mr. Randolph did get that Agreement drawn up, and we all signed it, and our course was set. I want to state that throughout our negotiations and subsequent dealings with Mr. Randolph, he worked hard on this deal and was straight up in living up to his part of the Agreement.

Well, what happened?

Craig Pena personally came up with the entire amount necessary to bring the account current, and continued to make all the other payments to Bowler Enterprises as agreed. He did a great job and fulfilled every promise that was made. Bowler

Enterprises, in turn, made the payments to AEL Financial, LLC per the terms of their Agreement.

And, on November 18, 2013, Bowler Enterprises sent the final lease/contract payment to AEL Financial, along with a separate check in the amount of one dollar and requested the transfer of free and clear title to all equipment that served as collateral for the contract to Bruce and Julie Bowler. This payment was paid as soon as Bowler Enterprises got AEL's invoice for that final payment, and did so advancing its own funds. We couldn't wait to pay this final payment and get title to the equipment. Craig followed up as promised and reimbursed us for the payment we had advanced, AEL lived up to their end of the agreement, and we all achieved a happy and successful conclusion to what could have been a disaster for everyone.

Just to clarify for any of you who might be wondering how we got "clear title" to that equipment—we didn't. What we did get was their release of their UCCC filing, which was the "lien" they had filed against the equipment, which, by their release of that lien, then effectively gave us clear title to what was actually already owned.

So the final debt had been paid.

What a ride.

The light has now, really and truly, been pulled in after us.

The End.

Chapter 19

THE POST SCRIPT

If you've made it to this point, you're obviously still with me, and I didn't bore you to tears, scare you to death, or leave you in the dust of the details and the stories. So let's talk about what this book is really all about.

It is *not* about quitting.

On January 3, 2012, I sent an e-mail to Jeff Brinen, my "bankruptcy" attorney.

The Subject: "Final Report."

Here, in part, is what that e-mail said:

> "Dear Jeff,
>
> This is just for your information, being sent as a courtesy to you to report on what I think has been a successfully completed "Self-Managed Liquidation."
>
> I thought you might want to see what two years of labor has accomplished. And, as you so adroitly pointed out to me when we first met in October of 2009, it did take "from one to two years." But you also said you thought it could work, and you were right about that.

> The real estate market and the economy were tough these past two years, or this may have been done closer to the one-year target. But, it is what it is, and all I can say is "Thank You" for your counsel, guidance and encouragement in assisting me when I set out on this adventure. It has truly been an experience. It has been so varied and interesting, filled with high highs and low lows and everything in between, that I have begun writing a book about it, entitled ***Into the Darkness,*** with the subtitle, **Yes, There Is a Time to Pull the Plug.**

As you can see from my e-mail, my original title was more about the emotions and feelings of what I was experiencing with the closing down of the company. The book title was later changed to help those who might want or need what's contained in the book to actually find it.

Jeff sent me a wonderful response back, in which he said:

> "I've had many clients decide to settle and pay their debts over time, rather than file bankruptcy. It's very commendable, but it rarely works out. In most cases, they come back and file bankruptcy. You're the exception, and it looks to me like you did an amazing job."

Then he went on to say:

> "Please let me know when you finish your book, as I'd like to buy a copy with your signature. I believe there's a strong market for a book as you describe, and there's also a market for your consulting services in this area. I have no expertise in marketing and sales, but I know there are many thousands of people who would pay you to help them

develop a plan to avoid bankruptcy. I'm frequently asked how it is that people/businesses can pay me when they're about to go bankrupt, and the fact is that they find a way. They would find a way to pay you, too."

Wow. Another awesome experience out of this odyssey.

I replied thanking Jeff for his great response and his encouragement on getting my book written and published.

I then shared with him the following insights:

"There are what I believe to be two keys to my being able to have gotten this [the self-managed liquidation] done:

1. **Recognizing that there is a "window of opportunity"** (and I have found that windows are generally pretty narrow!) where if you pull the plug, you have a fairly decent chance of pulling it off; but if you hang on and wait and *hope things will get better,* with really no chance that they will, you are toast. Somehow I figured out where my window was, and made the decision to close the business. You can't wait until everything is gone.

2. **Working your butt off and never giving up.** This became my full-time career for two years, and while I still had business things that I put together, etc., to keep money coming in and food on our table, this pretty much consumed me. You must be ready, willing, and able to truly dedicate yourself to its accomplishment.

That's a glimpse into my book, and the two biggest gems it will contain."

I concluded my reply with:

> "**Plus,** *make sure you get a great attorney who can tell things like they are and give you good direction and encouragement—like* you."

I promised him that he would be the first to hear from me when I got my book done. When I finally completed the original manuscript in August of 2016, I printed it out, put it into a notebook binder, and had the most wonderful experience of personally delivering it to Jeff and reminiscing about what we had gone through together. That was a sweet moment that I'll never forget.

This book is about knowing when to throw in the towel, about calling a spade a spade, about recognizing when there's nothing left that you can give to make something work, and then about having the guts to get rid of it, to close it down, and to take it through the processes that I have described.

And the second part of this book is about *never* quitting!!!

It's about doing everything in your power to go over any and all of the obstacles and stumbling blocks that *will* show up in front of you, and to never give in to those circumstances, but keep on truckin' and get 'er to the end, successfully.

Lastly, I want to share with you not only the overwhelming relief and gratitude that came from completing this journey, going into and through the darkness and having that beautiful light actually come in after me, but also the exhilaration that comes from conquering one's fears, and the ensuing, oh so powerful, self-confidence that truly is the father and mother of courage.

That is what this book is all about—and to help other people who find themselves in the same situation I was in, or who are facing any of life's difficult circumstances.

And this is what my book is hereby dedicated to.

EPILOGUE

At the end of it all, did I save time, money, and my sanity?

Absolutely!

Let's look at how this was.

Time

By going the route I did, I was able to get started right away selling the company assets. Even before we closed the doors, I had sold our most expensive equipment and shed our biggest debt. And within three months, all three major company divisions were sold and delivered, the structures were all set up to take care of our customers on future orders of product we had made for them, and the debts attributable to those divisions were gone.

The sale of the building housing our plant took a long time, but that was due to market conditions at the time. If we had been in a better real estate market environment, that would have gone much quicker and with more net proceeds out of a sale. Still, in spite of everything, it worked. And, I would emphatically state, it wouldn't have gone as well as it did, with the outcome we got, if I hadn't personally been involved taking care of each and every part of this liquidation.

Money

When you take a look at the fees that would have to have been funded for attorneys, court costs, procedures, time factors, etc., it is clear that in addition to the fact that we really didn't have the money to upfront the costs of a bankruptcy, we also saved a lot of money. In the end, it proved out that every cent we saved by taking care of things ourselves was critical to bringing our self-managed liquidation off successfully, and with something left over—mainly our home.

Sanity

Let's agree on this point: You built your business; who better to liquidate it? Who knows the business details like you do? Who knows the equipment and how it all works like you do? Who knows the customers and how you want them to be taken care of after the dust settles like you do? With the personal characteristics within you that encouraged you to build a business in the first place, how would it not be mentally better for you to be in control of all of these things and take care of the closure and liquidation of your company yourself?

As an entrepreneur, almost by definition, we are up for a challenge. Instead of watching attorneys and the courts determine the fate of our company, taking charge of handling the process is so much more in keeping with our inner selves. And, as I see how our products are even now still "coming off the line" through the businesses of those to whom we sold our equipment, inventory, and processes, and gave instructions to, in a way, Phoenix Custom Apparel still lives on.

Credit Rating

One other benefit that came out of all of the struggles is that, because of the way we were able to get everything taken care of, our credit ratings turned out to be pretty good, and we walked away still being able to answer "No" to the question: "Have you ever taken bankruptcy?" I know that's not always possible, and the world accepts taking bankruptcy when it is the only option, but remember: It may not be the only option available. Our experience has proven that.

ACKNOWLEDGMENTS

Now that I have taken you on this incredible journey, I want to acknowledge some special individuals who had a profound influence on one of the most difficult, learning, trying, and memorable experiences of my life.

First would be Paul Kluck, one of the premier commercial real estate brokers alive. I first met Paul when he sold me the office/warehouse building that housed Phoenix Custom Apparel, my apparel-manufacturing business, here in Denver, Colorado. He stayed friends with me over the nine years and nine months my business was alive, became my agent when we listed that same property for sale, counseled me and encouraged me at all times, and, most importantly, never stopped believing that I could actually pull off one of the most incredible business pursuits of my life.

Second would be Jeff Brinen, an attorney who specializes in bankruptcies and to whom I had the good fortune of being recommended by another bankruptcy attorney (which tells you something about what his colleagues think of him). Jeff took the time to go through the two options available to a businessman faced with how to deal with closing a business down, and he fully explained the differences between declaring bankruptcy and doing a "self-managed liquidation." He covered the pros and cons, the pitfalls, and the time and effort the second option would entail. He became my guide and expertly taught me and advised me as I wandered through the maze of dealing with a mountain of debt with less-than-adequate funding sources to take care of the creditors. He was another encourager, from beginning to end, and an awesome resource, without whom I am certain I would not have made it.

I also want to acknowledge my dear wife, Julie. I know that when we became husband and wife in June of 1961 we both had great hopes and dreams for the future. Our adventures over the years kind of reminds me of that great song performed by Glen Campbell and Bobby Gentry, entitled "My Elusive Dreams". And yet, here you are, still by my side, through all the ups and downs and the myriad events of our lives. You have endured it all, through thick and thin, and I would that I had not made you go through what you've gone through. Nevertheless, at the end of the day, I can at least say you were not encumbered with a boring life. Thank you for being there with me, through it all.

Lastly, I want to give a special recognition to my Executive Team of Matthew Bowler and Mary Tennien and our Board of Director Members Denis Iler and John Cowan, all of whom unequivocally and unanimously agreed that our best course of action was to close the company doors, regardless of the personal consequences.

STORYBOARD APPENDIX

Several of the colleagues I asked to read and evaluate my original manuscript suggested that I expand the concept of storyboarding, as that seemed to be recognized as an important management tool that helped in our successful closing down of Phoenix Custom Apparel.

It was a business tool that was revealed in a business seminar that I attended many years ago, put together and taught by Michael Vance, who had been the Idea and People Development Director for Walt Disney, and subsequently went out on his own with a company called Vance Creative Thinking System.

I still have the notebook that I put together from that seminar and refer to it frequently. The storyboarding concept, which was the process that Disney used to lay out the sequences necessary to produce an animated cartoon or movie, was expanded to be able to provide a great step-by-step pathway to bring to pass any business idea, problem, or concept. It was a process I've used successfully and continuously since learning it back in April of 1977.

The concept is wonderfully simple in its structure.

First, you find a wall where you can tape or pin up 3" × 5" cards, and leave the storyboard up until the project is completed.

You then define your Main Topic, and write it on a card at the top of the wall.

Underneath the Main Topic, you start putting up Headers. A Header is a major piece of what is needed to be addressed to accomplish the Topic. Those headers can run across the top of your storyboard or down one side. I like having them as the first row along the top.

Beneath each Header, you start making Subbers. A Subber is something that needs to be done to assist in accomplishing the Header. Right on the Subber, it is a good idea to put who is to accomplish that task and by what date. When the assigned person completes said task, they are to enter on the Subber the date it was completed.

If you have a complex Topic, you may need to then "turn the storyboard on its side," so to speak, where you treat each Header as a Topic, and each Subber becomes a Header, and then you put down the Subbers needed to complete those Headers. Just be careful that you don't go too deep, as it is easy to do that. I have found that, once you get to actual "action items," you've gone deep enough. Commonly, just one layer deep works.

See the following page for an example of a Storyboard structure.

With the closing of Phoenix Custom Apparel, our main TOPIC was "**CLOSING THE COMPANY DOWN**."

Each Header, as shown in the 3" × 5" cards across the top (when a specific Header is mentioned in this narrative, it will be shown in **bold** print), was to identify each major task that had to be addressed in closing down the company. Each Subber

TOPIC

HEADER HEADER HEADER HEADER

SUBBER SUBBER SUBBER SUBBER

below a Header, shown in the 3" × 5" cards going below each Header, was to identify each of the action items that needed to be performed to contribute to accomplishing the Header, and to identify which person was to take responsibility for performing the action item. Usually it is a good idea to put a completion date on each Subber, but since the action items needed to be done so quickly, dating the action items was not put on a lot of the cards in our storyboard.

With the plan set before us, we began taking the steps to accomplish each task.

Our first Header was entitled, **"When to Let Employees Go."** We all felt our first obligation was to let our staff know what was going to happen.

We began with Eric. We brought him in right away and told him that we were closing the company, and that there were to be no further sales put together (shown in the Storyboard as **"Accepting New Orders"**). We made it clear that no new orders were to be accepted after 2:00 p.m. on the 17th. That stopped any new orders from being generated that could take our production activities beyond our goal of being deliverable by month's end. We then went over all the sales in the pipeline (shown in the Storyboard as **"Work Orders in Process"**) and made the determination of how to complete and deliver them. This was important, and we felt that all of the orders in the system could be completed by September 25 (which was a Friday) so that we could ship the orders on or before September 30, with the desired result being that September 30 would be the last payday for our production personnel. After this discussion with Eric, it was agreed that his last day would be September 18.

We then called a meeting of all of the employees of the company and let them know that the company was going to close down by the end of the month. We let each of them know when we expected their last day to be, as different ones were to be let go sooner than others. We immediately began laying off people that we would not be needing to handle the production of the remaining orders in the pipeline, and then we followed the structured layoff schedule as the orders were finished up. Everything was designed to keep our payroll expenses down as low as possible and to also be able to make sure we had sufficient funds to pay people for the work they did.

We discussed providing Letters of Recommendation for those who wanted one, and also had contacted our accountant to receive advice on how to properly handle the details of the terminations.

Our biggest customer and affiliation relationship was with the National Hot Rod Association (seen on the Storyboard as **"Affiliate Notifications"**). We had fulfilled our obligations to them, and there were no unfulfilled needs to be coming from them other than the ability to get Champions Jackets manufactured. We knew we could work with NHRA to help provide guidance and other items to another company so that the winners' jackets wouldn't be a problem going forward. So, right after our storyboarding meeting, I called my liaison at NHRA and advised that we were closing down the company. After a shocked response, we had a good conversation on how this could all be pulled off without a hitch, and while we were both sad to see our relationship and activities ending, we knew that this could all be done without any problems. We then used our remaining full-page ads in *National Dragster* (see the Header entitled **"Publicity for Purchasers"**) to notify customers that we were closing down Phoenix Custom Apparel and to advertise companies that we later made deals with to take on divisions of our production lines where our customers could go to get future orders filled.

Then came the Header **"Sale of Company."** As I mentioned earlier, while the conventional business wisdom that creating bigger businesses with a variety of goods and services (known as synergy) would result in the creation of a better and more-valuable business, this didn't work well for us in closing the company down. In the end, it turned out that selling off the individual "pieces" or divisions of our company gave us the quickest sales and the most financial benefit from those sales.

Under the Header **"Customer Notifications,"** I was given the assignment to create a company statement that we would use not only in the *National Dragster* ad but also would be posted on our website. That would give notification of our shutdown and also prevent further orders from being placed. A natural Header in this arena of dealing with customers was **"Collection of Accounts Receivable,"** so that we could get as much funds in hand as possible to take care of current and ongoing obligations.

Under the Headers **"Follow Up Orders for Customers"** and **"Customer Last Requests,"** we started putting the structures together for where we could send them and make sure that items like embroidery digitizing that customers had paid for, and art/design work that we had done for customers, would all be available to them so that they could continue to get the products they had been getting from us. That was also worked into the **"Handling Telephone Inquiries"** Header; plus, it was part of the negotiations I conducted when selling divisions of our company to those purchasers who were taking over our firesuit manufacturing (shown under the **"Special Items"** Header, and the Talk to Dennis Taylor Subber), our sublimation equipment and services, and our embroidery equipment and services.

One of the Storyboard Headers was **"PRI Show,"** The Performance Racing Industry trade show was the most important trade show event of the year and was very expensive. Space and hotel accommodations had to be reserved well in advance, and money was on the line. We had to cancel all the arrangements and do it quickly. This was assigned to Jeanne, another daughter of ours and our Office Manager, which she accomplished immediately. She took care of many of the logistical action items in the storyboard.

The **"Canceling of Services"** Header for canceling our toll-free telephone line, our Comcast Internet services, canceling e-mail addresses, accounts with FedEx and UPS, and attendant services were all discussed as to when these services could be terminated without causing us a problem, and then taken care of by assignment.

Since we owned our building, which had a first and a second mortgage on it, one of the Headers was entitled **"Real Estate."** The Subbers under this Header dealt with me seeing if our next-door neighbor, who had expressed a slight interest at one point in time about acquiring our building, was still interested. It also involved me contacting my real estate agent, Paul Kluck, about listing our property for sale and for me to go personally visit with Colorado Housing and Finance Authority, who was the holder of our first mortgage, and Preferred Lending Partners, who serviced our SBA second mortgage. I contacted these individuals within days of our meeting. The meeting with Paul Kluck resulted in me setting up a meeting with a bankruptcy attorney to address the best way to close down the company and deal with all of our creditors, etc.

Another large Header was "**Handling Vendors.**" We had many vendors that we purchased fabrics and other supplies from, and we needed to make sure that any orders for product that weren't yet delivered were canceled, to see what we still owed on items received and to negotiate with those where we had any appreciable inventory in stock to see if we could return said inventory to them and get refunds.

As you might gather from perusing the process we went through, this system is a great way to make sure that you stay on track, that you can move quickly and in a highly coordinated fashion, and especially so if you have multiple members of a team working on the Topic, that everyone can keep on top of how it is moving along, since it is to be updated as assignments are accomplished. It also is very helpful in keeping details from falling through the cracks, even more so if the storyboard is created using the members of the team who will be in charge of accomplishing the Topic. I have found it to be a wonderful tool to create something quickly, even when it was just me being the one working on the Topic and bringing it all to a conclusion. There is no better road map you can find.

ABOUT THE AUTHOR

Bruce Bowler was born in Washington, D.C. in 1941. His family moved to Denver at an early age, where he was raised and educated. He received his BSBA degree cum laude from the University of Denver, for which he was admitted to the Beta Gamma Sigma Honorary Society.

He joined his father's mortgage banking company while still in school, graduated from the Mortgage Bankers Association of America School of Mortgage Banking, and embarked on a forty year career in the mortgage banking industry. During that career, he worked at various financial institutions in Denver, culminating in being half owner of Universal Lending Corporation for fourteen years. During his career, he was appointed to the Board of Directors of the Colorado Housing and Finance Authority by two of Colorado's Governors, and served on that Board for fourteen years, one of which he served as Chairman of the Board. He also served in leadership roles in the Colorado Mortgage Lenders Association, serving as President of that organization for one term.

He also served on the Board of the Rocky Mountain College of Art & Design, was appointed to Governor Hickenlooper's

Wildfire Task Force, and served on national and regional councils to the Federal National Mortgage Association.

He received numerous designations and awards during his mortgage banking career, including recognitions from the U.S. Department of Housing and Urban Development and the Veterans Administration, and awards recognizing his leadership and dedication to public-private partnerships in support of the free enterprise system, and the coveted CMLA Lifetime Achievement Award presented in 2015.

In 1968, Bruce took a three-year sabbatical from mortgage banking to accept the position of Division Director of the Northwest Division of the National Hot Rod Association, and relocated his family to Vancouver, Washington. Shortly after taking on that assignment, having been thoroughly acclimated to using FHA and VA manuals, he authored the first NHRA Drag Strip Manager's OPERATIONS GUIDE. That Guide was approved by NHRA's legal counsel, its executive vice president, and Wally Parks, founder and President of NHRA, and Bruce was given authorization to produce the Guide for distribution to all NHRA sanctioned tracks in the United States and Canada. In 2001, he received NHRA's Pioneer Award in recognition of the contributions he made to the sport of drag racing.

Bruce then returned to Denver to finish up his career in mortgage banking.

In 1998 he then sold his interest in Universal Lending Corporation, and began a semi-professional career in drag racing, owning and driving a nitro-methane-burning Top Alcohol Dragster. While campaigning the race car throughout the central and western United States, he started the apparel manufacturing company known as Phoenix Custom Apparel.

After closing Phoenix down in September of 2009, he started up Bowler Enterprises, to continue to provide custom-designed apparel to previous customers, through an affiliation with a manufacturer in China. He also dusted off his real estate license that he had held since 1973, and became an active real estate broker, providing listing and buyer agency services.

In addition to those businesses that he continues to own and operate, he composes and records his own music, and, with the completion of this book, has now become a published author.

Bruce married Julie Botterill in 1961. They have seven children, who have thus far given their parents some twenty-one grandchildren and eight great-grandchildren.

I hope you enjoyed this book. Would you do me a favor?

Like all authors, I rely on online reviews to encourage future sales. Your opinion is invaluable. Would you take a few moments now to share your assessment of my book on Amazon or any other book-review website you prefer? If you prefer, you could just communicate with me through my website: brucebowler.com. Your opinion will help the book marketplace become more transparent and useful to all.

Thank you so much!

www.ingramcontent.com/pod-product-compliance
Lightning Source LLC
Chambersburg PA
CBHW021055210326
41598CB00016B/1217